Overcoming disadvantage

Overcoming disadvantage was commissioned and written as a response to a working paper and report published by the Joseph Rowntree Foundation in February 2003. All three can be downloaded free from the JRF website (www.jrf.org.uk/bookshop), or purchased from our distributor, YPS, on 01904 430033.

Tackling disadvantage
A 20-year enterprise
David Darton, Donald Hirsch and Jason Strelitz
A concise review of how poverty could be substantially reduced in Britain over the next two decades, this report is based on a wide-ranging review of the research evidence and a series of seminars and discussions with key academics, journalists and policy makers.

The report begins by identifying some fundamental causes of poverty and disadvantage, and looks at who is most affected. It sets out the key issues in six areas – education, family poverty, geographic disadvantage, income poverty, housing and long-term care. It highlights the problems that need to be tackled, and the long-term goals that policy needs to adopt. Some of the consequent directions policy makers might take are illustrated with examples of possible policy as a stimulus for further thinking.

Tackling UK poverty and disadvantage in the twenty-first century
Edited by David Darton and Jason Strelitz
This study provides background detail to support the working paper *Tackling disadvantage*.

The report includes chapters on the future for education, families, housing, long-term care, regional disadvantage, and income. There are supplementary chapters on key questions that need to be addressed, and background papers underpinning the arguments.

Overcoming disadvantage
An agenda for the next 20 years

IPPR (Institute for Public Policy Research), Social Market Foundation, Policy Exchange, Scottish Council Foundation, and Institute of Welsh Affairs

Introduction by Nicholas Timmins

The **Joseph Rowntree Foundation** has commissioned this project as part of its programme of research and innovative development projects, which it hopes will be of value to policy makers, practitioners and service users. The facts presented and views expressed in this report are, however, those of the authors and not necessarily those of the Foundation.

Joseph Rowntree Foundation
The Homestead
40 Water End
York YO30 6WP
Website: www.jrf.org.uk

First published 2004 by the Joseph Rowntree Foundation

ISBN 1 85935 142 5 (paperback)
     1 85935 143 3 (pdf: available at www.jrf.org.uk)

A CIP catalogue record for this report is available from the British Library.

Designed by Adkins Design (www.adkinsdesign.co.uk)

Further copies of this report, or any other JRF publication, can be obtained either from the JRF website (www.jrf.org.uk/bookshop/) or from our distributor, York Publishing Services Ltd, 64 Hallfield Road, Layerthorpe, York YO31 7ZQ (Tel: 01904 430033).

| Contents

Notes on contributors

Nicholas Timmins is Public Policy Editor of the *Financial Times* and author of the award-winning *The five giants: A biography of the welfare state* (HarperCollins 2001), now in its second edition.

The **Institute for Public Policy Research (ippr)** is a progressive think-tank established in 1988. It aims to bridge the political divide between the social democratic and liberal traditions, the intellectual divide between academia and the policy making establishment and the cultural divide between government and civil society. It is a research institute which aims to provide innovative and credible policy solutions. **Sue Regan** is Head of Social Policy and **Peter Robinson** is Senior Economist at ippr. Website: www.ippr.org.uk.

The **Social Market Foundation** was established in 1989 to provide a source of innovative social and economic policy ideas. Its current work reflects a commitment to understanding how individuals, society and the state can work together to achieve the common goal of creating a just and free society. The SMF is involved in current debates on education, health, welfare reform and family policy. **Roger Wicks** is a Research Fellow of the Social Market Foundation. Website: www.smf.co.uk.

Policy Exchange was launched in April 2002 to develop fresh solutions to Britain's social problems. It is exploring ways of extending the benefits of strong communities whilst limiting state interference. Policy Exchange is working towards a society in which families, local neighbourhoods and voluntary and faith groups are able to flourish and in which people who are currently disadvantaged are offered genuine opportunities. **Nicholas Hillman** is a Research Fellow of Policy Exchange. Website: www.policyexchange.org.uk.

The **Scottish Council Foundation** was established in 1997. It is an independent think-tank working with government, business and communities, developing new thinking in a range of social, economic and governance issues. It is a charitable trust funded through a network of principal supporters and project-based income. **Jim McCormick** is the Director of the Scottish Council Foundation, **Fiona Spencer** is Programme Director, and **Corinna Gamble** is Research Fellow. Website: www.scottishcouncilfoundation.org.

The **Institute of Welsh Affairs** is an independent, membership-based policy think-tank that promotes informed debate and new thinking on economic, social and political issues. It was founded in the mid-1980s. The Institute publishes a regular journal (*Agenda*), policy papers and research reports. A branch network across Wales organises seminars, conferences and other events throughout the year. **John Osmond** is the Director, and **Jessica Mugaseth** Research Officer, of the Institute of Welsh Affairs. Website: www.iwa.org.uk.

Foreword

Last year the Joseph Rowntree Foundation published *Tackling disadvantage: A 20-year enterprise*, a working paper intended to stimulate discussion about action needed in the long term to tackle poverty and social exclusion. While scrutinising a wide range of policy areas, it was built around one central assertion: that a mission to progressively reduce poverty in the next 20 years is affordable and can be achieved, provided the political will exists to carry it out.

Now, as the Foundation starts to celebrate its centenary year, we are pleased to take the dialogue about overcoming disadvantage a stage forward with this latest, challenging report. Bringing together five essays commissioned from leading think-tanks, it launches the next, essential task of finding new ideas and policy proposals in response to the old and often intractable issues that still need to be addressed. Three of the contributing organisations – the IPPR, Social Market Foundation and Policy Exchange – were invited to participate because their standpoints range from the centre-left to the centre-right of British politics. Our invitations to the Scottish Council Foundation and the Institute of Welsh Affairs flowed from a complementary desire to capture fresh thinking and perspectives among the devolved 'home nations'.

Few who read the five contrasting contributions will doubt that we have succeeded in our aim. Each chapter brings its own, distinctive viewpoint and innovative suggestions abound. Yet while avoiding significant overlap, many of the proposals can be seen to dovetail in a way that is potentially very constructive. Impressively – as Nicholas Timmins, Public Policy Editor of the *Financial Times*, notes in his introduction and overview – the essays pave the way for future consensus among the main political parties on the value of tackling poverty. This would have seemed unthinkable a decade ago.

One hundred years ago, our founder Joseph Rowntree gave us the objective of searching out the underlying causes of social ills and finding new solutions. While the nature and scale of the social problems we confront today are different, his core concerns with impoverished lives and unsatisfactory neighbourhoods remain central to our work. For that reason, it has been decided that the Foundation's culminating two-day conference at the end of this centenary year will focus on the twin themes of 'poverty' and 'place'. Taken with our own working paper, the contributions to this report will ensure that the debate about long-term policy prescriptions can be carried forward at the highest level of informed and imaginative thinking.

Richard Best
Director, Joseph Rowntree Foundation
February 2004

Introduction and overview

Towards consensus?

Nicholas Timmins, Public Policy Editor, Financial Times

Back in March 1999, Tony Blair set the still-new Labour government a challenge more specific and arguably bolder than any previous administration had attempted in the previous half-century – to end child poverty within a generation.

As part of the preparations for its centenary in 2004 the Joseph Rowntree Foundation has taken that proposition one step further. It is asking how poverty and social disadvantage can be tackled over the next 20 years, not just for families with children, but for all: those who are without children and below retirement age, and those who are now in retirement.

The scale of what that involves was set out in *Tackling disadvantage*, the Foundation's 2003 working paper, which spelt out the current position and calculated the resources which might be needed to achieve such an aim.

The difficulty of reaching that achievement is already illustrated in the continuing debate on whether Labour will hit, miss, or just miss the first milestone down the road to its more limited child poverty target: whether the billions of pounds so far injected into tax credits and Income Support rates, together with a wide range of other welfare to work initiatives and new programmes such as *Sure Start,* will have succeeded in lifting a million children out of poverty by 2004.

The essays in this publication are from five think-tanks invited to comment on the JRF's consultation document and then go further by producing their own ideas and policy proposals for achieving the bigger 20-year objective.

The organisations represented may not cover the full range of the political spectrum. But they offer a pretty broad sweep, bringing views from left and right, from Scotland and Wales; and from those who see the issue in geographic and community terms as well as from those who analyse the problems in terms of individuals and groups within society.

The first point that stands out before all others is that there is now a common currency in the debate. Poverty and social disadvantage are seen, across the political spectrum, as live issues that need to be tackled.

The essay from Policy Exchange by Nicholas Hillman, until recently the key researcher to David Willetts, the Shadow Work and Pensions Secretary, is a far cry from the Conservatives' headline attitudes of the 1980s and early 1990s. Margaret Thatcher may have been somewhat misrepresented by being only partially quoted in her famous statement when Prime Minister that 'there is no such thing as society'. But the views reflected in Hillman's essay are a far cry from the previous Conservative government's refusal, to the point almost of denial, to acknowledge that health inequalities existed, and from the stance adopted by John Moore in his 1988 speech, 'The end of the line for poverty'. Even Hillman's chosen title, 'Condemning a little less and understanding a little more', is a calculated reversal of a pronouncement once made by Mrs Thatcher's successor, John Major.

At the time of writing, Michael Howard had just assumed the Conservative Party leadership. The proof of the rhetoric will come in pre-election policies. But the language of 'one nation' Conservatism, which has long acknowledged a serious concern for the least well-off, has been discernible in his early pronouncements. Thus the chances of some degree of consensus about aims in tackling poverty and disadvantage, if not about means, appears higher than for many years – at least for the time being.

Even so, the essays in this collection raise the question of how boldly those shared aims can and will be stated politically. Labour has enunciated its goal on child poverty clearly enough. To make progress, it has sharply raised the children's rates in Income Support, boosted Child Benefit, and introduced the Child Tax Credit. Moreover, Labour's policies have produced small percentage losses in income at the top end of the income distribution. This is redistribution by any measure. But as pointed out by Sue Regan and Peter Robinson of the IPPR, this has been done largely by stealth. It is not a result that Labour appears inclined to boast about for fear of frightening the horses of so-called 'middle England'. The 'R' word seems to be banned from Labour's lexicon. Yet doing good by stealth, as Ruth Lister has observed, runs the risk of not being seen to do good at all. That in turn raises the question of how far a consensus among the electorate has been built, or can be built, for the longer-term aims.

In addition, Labour has concentrated its redistribution on lower income pensioners and on children (although, of course, where children gain, the families they live in gain too). Politically, such a strategy may be sound. Pensioners and children are plainly seen by the electorate as more deserving than single people below retirement age, or couples without children. Labour clearly hopes the measures it has taken and the language in which they have been cast will 'lock in' the aspiration of ending child poverty, ensuring it would survive a change of government. But if the long-term aim is to embrace the broader objective of tackling social disadvantage, questions must inevitably arise as to how far existing welfare to work programmes – with their mix of sticks and carrots – can assist those without children who are poor and disadvantaged.

This, in turn, raises the big issue of how far benefits can provide an adequate floor of income for younger childless people without damaging work incentives in a world where there is downward pressure – despite the minimum wage – on pay rates for unskilled workers. The relationship between wages, in-work benefits (now cast in the form of tax credits) and out-of-work benefits has long been fraught. At the moment there is little sign that, for those without children, it is getting any easier.

Furthermore, despite significant transfers to the bottom 20 per cent of the population since 1997, it appears that the widening of the gap in income between rich and poor has at best been halted rather than the gap narrowed. It happens that the break in the trend of ever increasing income inequality predated Labour's arrival in office, its higher spending, and its redistributive measures. But it remains an open question how far globalisation and technological change will continue to spread the income distribution wider – and what the effect will be on a poverty line set at 60 per cent of median income. No JRF report would ever be complete without a recommendation for further research. But a better understanding of what is happening here, and what is likely to happen, is undoubtedly needed.

Other big themes that emerge from the essays are the need to tackle not just unemployment but economic inactivity. For while Labour's redistribution to the out-of-work has helped, it is rising employment rates and economic activity that have had the biggest impact on the least well-off. Yet here Labour's welfare to work programme appears to have lost its head of steam. The energy and drive that went into the New Deal programmes for young people and lone parents have not been replicated in similar, large scale, programmes for the growing numbers on disability benefits. Surveys repeatedly show that large numbers of them wish to work. Equally, as Sue Regan and Peter Robinson note, the make-up of people on disability benefits is changing. No longer does physical disability from industrial or other injuries dominate the inflow to disability benefits. These days mental health problems and stress are key causes of claims. A proportion of such claims will involve intractable mental illness. But a proportion may be far more amenable to treatment and behavioural programmes that could help engineer a return to work.

Constructing such intensive programmes is not easy. They will need to cut across health, benefit and social care responsibilities within both central and local government and the NHS. In the employment zones and some other parts of its welfare to work programme, the government has shown considerable imagination in using private and voluntary sector suppliers – approaches from which the public sector has been able to learn. But there seems to be no comparable drive to try a sufficiently wide range of innovative programmes for the sick and disabled. This despite it being an area where imagination and experimentation needs to be applied, and where the public and private sectors may be able to achieve more together than either can separately. That applies both to early intervention to divert people from the need to claim benefits in the first place, and to rehabilitation for those already claiming. A second generation of welfare to work programmes in this area is badly needed.

Looking further at the micro-measures needed to tackle social disadvantage, it is noticeable that several of the essays highlight the need to use the Social Fund more imaginatively. A word of warning is needed here. The Social Fund is heavily criticised. But in one important respect it has been a success. By operating on a closed budget and offering much of its help in the form of loans, it put an end to what had been a running sore for governments of all colours for 30 years: the seemingly inexorable growth in the various forms of extra payments made through what was then called Supplementary Benefit. Any reform is therefore likely to have to stick within the existing formula. Nonetheless, both the Policy Exchange proposals and those from Roger Wicks at the Social Market Foundation see an extended role for the fund – both as a means of easing the transition into work and as a means of preventing over-indebtedness.

Poverty, after all, is not just about income. It involves assets, costs and debts, and the Social Fund is a far better borrowing bet than most commercial means of borrowing, and certainly better than borrowing from loan sharks. Asset building is the newest idea in welfare reform. It has the advantage of being an idea that is of neither the left nor the right. It can appeal to both, as evidenced by debate and action in the United States, and in the interest that David Willetts has shown in the idea. The Labour government has made a start with the Child Trust Fund and the pilots of the 'savings gateway'. Both, at present, are modest. Even if the former succeeds in its aim of encouraging saving – a potentially important behavioural change – the full payback remains 20 years away. Yet what may be most remarkable about the Child Trust Fund is not the modest scale on which it is being launched, but that the idea survived at all at a time when government spending is coming under pressure. Grander ideas debated here include making a one-off payment to young people at age 18 – presumably introducing this before the Child Trust Fund programme matures – and exploring asset building for social housing tenants.

Reducing the cost of debt, and the other costs of poverty, is an equally important theme and it is highlighted in the contribution from Jim McCormick and colleagues at the Scottish Council Foundation (SCF). As they rightly point out, energy, food, transport, insurance and financial services all tend to cost the poor more than the better-off. Reducing the costs of poverty may do nothing to reduce the proportion of households living below the poverty line. However, reducing such costs by a given percentage would produce the same rise in living standards, in terms of disposable income, as an equivalent increase in benefits or earnings. The SCF highlights some important initiatives in this area such as 'insure with rent' payments that give access to home insurance at group rates to social housing tenants. It also makes proposals in other areas, for example for reducing food bills, that will be subject to more debate about whether central and local government have the competence to manage such markets.

Some of the Scottish thinking clearly sees poverty in terms of communities and areas, and other essays broadly welcome the thinking in the original JRF document which acknowledged a distinct regional aspect to social disadvantage. That comes across most strongly in John Osmond and Jessica Mugaseth's contribution from the Institute of Welsh Affairs (IWA). The extent to which poverty reduction in Wales is seen as an issue for communities highlights one of the dilemmas for policy: that while poverty is heavily concentrated in certain areas, it remains true that across much of the UK most poor people don't live in the poorest areas. In Wales, the particular problems of the valleys counter that argument, and the picture of distrust of local authorities as agents for change, coupled with the need to build initiatives from the ground up, comes across strongly.

Housing too is an issue that requires a regional and area-based view as well as a national one. Of all the big social security issues, Housing Benefit has been subjected to the least reform to date by the Labour government. Pilots are under way for a localised housing allowance, which a growing part of the policy community now believes may offer the route to a long-term solution. The need to prove the approach, however, will make progress slow. Aside from the fierce debate about housing growth in the South East, it also seems clear that any reform of Housing Benefit needs to reach not just tenants but homeowners on low incomes if it is to play a stronger role in combating poverty. One idea that might be worth exploring in the case of older home owners is paying the benefit as an, at least, partial charge on the home – in effect making it a form of equity release.

Interestingly, comparisons between the essays raise a number of issues that the JRF's original consultation document did not directly address. For example, Nicholas Hillman queries the impact of immigration on poverty and the effect it can have on the unskilled or deskilled indigenous population. Those risks, in turn, have to be set against the willingness of older unemployed men from traditional industries to accept what they see as 'women's work' or jobs that aren't 'real jobs' – attitudes that may be dying out, but which the IWA makes clear still remain an issue in Wales. Moreover a wide range of service industries will always demand a pool of semi- or unskilled labour – the sort of work that first generation immigrants have often been willing to accept as their first step to establishing a new life.

Three other big themes emerge from JRF's original paper and the essays. One is how to develop welfare to work programmes so that they enhance skills and employability, not just for those out of work, but for those who move into it. Learning accounts and intermediate labour markets that can be allowed to operate while people retain benefit entitlements are still relatively embryonic ideas for building human capital that appear to merit more development.

Second it is clear that the perennial debate between universalism and means testing is far from dead. Labour, having been in the past an arch-opponent of means testing, has in practice achieved much of its redistribution in office by using it. There has been a genuine attempt to tackle the complications and stigma of claiming means-tested benefits, not least through the creation and language of tax credits. Yet the critics, some of whose voices can he heard in these essays, are unconvinced, insisting that the price has been unacceptable complexity. And in the case of pensions, there are certainly strong arguments that the Pension Credit, while a clear gain for today's poorer pensioners, has made decisions about saving far harder for today's lower income workers. Add to that the recent falls in stock-markets, greater longevity and the underfunding of pension schemes and there is a feeling that Britain's pension system is at a crossroads. Travelling further down the means-tested road is likely to lead to greater compulsion to save. The alternative route would be for the basic state pension to be rebuilt and turned into something closer to a participation, or even a 'citizenship', pension. All this would be at the price of scrapping the second state pension and, in all probability, raising the state retirement age as well. Either approach carries implications for people on lower incomes that are likely to shape the mathematics of poverty – either through longer working (or non-working) lives before pensionable age is reached, or through compulsory pension contributions that will affect wages at lower income levels and may well impact on work incentives.

Finally there is the question of the fiscal context for any action to tackle poverty and disadvantage over the next 20 years. Recent history suggests public spending in the UK remains fixed by an iron electoral law which rules that it will not rise much above 40 to 42 per cent of GDP, despite some variation with the economic cycle. This heavily limits the room for straightforward redistribution. It emphasises the need for welfare to work programmes to demonstrate net economic and social gains, not just good intentions and limited impacts. And it underlines the fact that whatever policy tools are chosen – and a range of them are discussed in this book – a powerful political case will have to be made to convince the electorate that tackling social disadvantage is in the interests of all.

The JRF consultation paper argues that the mission is 'a tough but affordable' one. The Foundation calculates that the poverty gap could be closed if the income of the poorest rose for 20 years at the same rate as the most affluent enjoyed during the 1980s. However, on the Foundation's own figures, that would require the income of the bottom 10 per cent to rise at three times the rate enjoyed by the top 60 per cent of the population for two decades. Such a shift over such a sustained period could only be achieved with a more powerful political accord than yet exists. Building that consensus is as much of a challenge as designing the policy tools to deliver it.

1 | Loud and clear

An open and persistent poverty strategy

Sue Regan and Peter Robinson, IPPR (Institute for Public Policy Research)

Introduction

How do we tackle poverty in the next 20 years?

The central question of the Joseph Rowntree Foundation's *Tackling disadvantage* study is far from easy to answer. The persistence of poverty in the face of overall growing prosperity in Britain is a huge challenge. The current government has put tackling poverty and social exclusion at the heart of its reform agenda, with the historic pledge to eradicate child poverty within a generation confirming its commitment. While many important policy measures have been taken forward, it is widely recognised that more effort, further resources, new ideas and a more convincing long-term strategy will be needed if the goal of tackling poverty is to be achieved. Looking at a 20-year horizon, what steps are needed to head off potential future social problems and to tackle the poverty and disadvantage already blighting the lives of too many of our citizens and communities?

Priorities for action

Tackling disadvantage rises to this challenge but ultimately falls short on providing a comprehensive strategy for success. We suggest more is needed. Our response comments on the study's analysis and proposed policy solutions. We then put forward three interlinked 'priorities for action' that should sit alongside and will complement JRF's four principles. Our analysis highlights some new

21

policies but also, and crucially, a means of galvanising the necessary support to make change happen. These priorities for action are:

- mobilising support;
- redesigning a welfare contract;
- empowering individuals across the life cycle.

Analysis of the problem and suggested solutions
Recognising the break in trends from the early 1990s

The analysis of the problem in *Tackling disadvantage* is deficient and perhaps overly pessimistic in one important respect. It does not recognise that since the early 1990s there has been an important break in the trends towards greater wage and income inequality in the UK, in contrast to the very sharp rises in inequality that took place from the late 1970s, through the 1980s and into the early 1990s.

Over the last decade:

- wage inequality has stopped increasing in the UK (though it has not fallen);
- the gap in earnings between the well-qualified and the less well-qualified has stopped widening (though it has not narrowed);
- inequality in original income, or the income derived from the market, has stopped rising (though it has not fallen).

So during the period that has seen the most fevered debates about the supposedly remorseless impact of forces such as 'globalisation' and technological change, the worst outcomes ascribed to those forces have been tempered. If we ally this observation to the one repeatedly made by Tony Atkinson, that the sharp increases in income inequality and relative poverty seen in the UK and the US between the late

1970s and early 1990s were not mirrored in many other OECD countries, we should question the argument that there are trends in market economies that are inevitably leading to wider inequality.

This break in trend in the UK in the 1990s is significantly under-researched. The work by John Hills documenting and trying to explain the trends from the late 1970s to the mid 1990s is looking increasingly out of date.[1] This is surely one area for further research that the JRF should make a priority.

Choosing to tackle poverty

Tackling disadvantage debunks the theory that rising prosperity 'trickles down' to the poor, but does not give an answer to why a prosperous country such as the UK has not eradicated poverty. There is a fairly straightforward answer to this question. We have not eradicated poverty because as a country we have chosen not to do so. Indeed, the study shows very clearly that affordability is not the problem. It is a New Labour axiom that social justice and economic success must go together.[2] However, the evidence does not support this. Social justice and economic success in a modern industrial economy are largely independent of one another and each nation must choose how much social justice to pursue alongside any degree of economic success. This does not reduce the complexity and scale of the challenge, but much of this response explores how to enable this country to make the choice of furthering social justice and tackling poverty.

A welcome regional perspective

The analysis of the social, economic and demographic trends and their consequences illustrates accurately the scale of disadvantage and its continuation into the future unless a concerted poverty-elimination strategy is enacted. Particularly welcome in the analysis is the recognition of regional inequalities – an issue too often neglected in social and economic policy. The variation in employment rates between regions is stark. The North East, Wales and Northern Ireland have less than 70 per cent of working age adults in employment. Similarly, housing problems must be looked at in a regional context. It is now widely recognised that different strategies are needed for tackling areas of low demand and neighbourhood abandonment in the North and Midlands and for alleviating high demand and homelessness in much of the South. In policy terms what is still missing is a strong regional policy which focuses on raising employment in lagging regions and doing this not just through supply-side measures but also with policies aiming at increasing the number of jobs.[3]

Disability, mental health and complex need

As the study acknowledges, disabled people are more likely to be poor – but why is this? Disabled people are more likely to suffer poverty and disadvantage because they are more likely to be out of work and to be reliant on state benefits. In 2003, around 2.7 million people claimed incapacity benefits. Since 1997, during the period largely characterised by a healthy and stable economy, the number of people claiming incapacity benefits has continued to increase. The total now represents significantly more people than the combined total of lone parents and unemployed people on benefits and is highly concentrated regionally. Given the important impact that being in employment has on reducing poverty and social exclusion, the low employment rate is neither good for disabled people nor good for the wider economy and society. This has historically been a sensitive issue for government. But surveys consistently show that many disabled people want to work – there are well over 1 million disabled people who want to work but are not working.

The current government has responded to this but it is still the case that the scale of activity and resources that have been committed is being dwarfed by the scale of the problem. We think this should be a priority for government and a high profile campaign is needed to help disabled people who want to work to get into work. This must start with a new account of disability.[4] Over time, the nature of disability and the profile of the disabled population have changed. Disabled people are a highly diverse group and they include people who were born disabled as well as the majority who became disabled during their working lives. Crucially, a decade ago muscular skeletal or cardiovascular problems were the most commonly cited as reasons for not being able to work. Now mental health issues, often linked to workplace stress, dominate.

A response to the trend of increasing mental illness has to be part of an anti-poverty strategy. Given JRF's first principle of increasing the extent to which poorer households benefit from the market economy, mental illness represents a huge challenge. You are far less likely to be working if you have a mental health problem than if you suffer from any other condition. An anti-poverty strategy must also be able to reach the most excluded and particularly those with complex needs. Mental health issues linked to alcohol or drug abuse and manifesting themselves in joblessness and homelessness represent a complexity of need that public policy currently finds it very difficult to respond to. Even social care agencies struggle to recognise and respond to the holistic nature of people's needs.

New medicine and a new politics

Overall, we concur with *Tackling disadvantage*'s principles and suggested solutions. Much of the strategy implies that the response to persistent poverty should be to ratchet up the intensity of existing policies. Tax credits should be made more generous, the minimum wage increased, levels of spending on programmes such as *Sure Start* increased. There is much to be gained from this. There are, however, both policy and political reasons for thinking that this 'same medicine, higher dosage' approach, taken on its own, will not achieve a sustainable shift towards reducing disadvantage.

In policy terms, there are a number of areas which are currently underexploited. These include the lack of a radical agenda on generating more employment in disadvantaged regions, timidity in tax reform and genuinely empowering people to be active citizens. We explore some of these below. Politically, *Tackling disadvantage* is perhaps optimistic about the scope for direct redistributive taxation in the absence of strong public support. This leads to our first priority for action – mobilising support.

Mobilising support

Stealthy spending

The Chancellor currently has a big problem – a commitment to eradicate child poverty but public support that is silent. It would be fair to say that this is a problem, at least partly, of the government's own making. The government has met with some criticism not for its attempts to alleviate poverty, but for the manner in which it embarked on this agenda – namely by stealth.[5] Once the Chancellor was freed of his commitment to stay within the previous government's spending plans, subsequent budgets have been notably progressive. Those at the bottom of the income scale have made significant gains while those at the top have made small losses. Yet the Chancellor and his colleagues have consistently denied that this constitutes an explicit policy of redistribution. The 'r' word has essentially been banned from the New Labour lexicon. And as Ruth Lister has pointed out, 'doing good by stealth has the disadvantage of not being seen to be doing good.'

Since much of the progress has been made through largely technical and little-trumpeted changes in the tax/benefit system, this has not set the stage for further reform. Less visible forms of redistribution are politically attractive in the short term but do make more explicit reform more difficult in the longer term. Not only are there limits to the amount of reform which can be achieved by stealth, in the tighter fiscal situation we are now entering there will be no shortage of commentators questioning the wisdom of spending on further measures to reduce relative poverty. How do we respond to this pressure: technical reports setting out the debilitating impact of poverty on life chances have not yet translated into a popular political narrative. In the period after 1997 there was much hope pinned to the government's commitment to an annual poverty audit which would both galvanise public support and act as a 'self embarrassment too',[6] but the government's *Opportunity for all* report has failed to fulfil its promise.

A definition of poverty

What is needed is a means of benchmarking progress in tackling poverty which can both keep politicians to account and garner public support. We agree that the best single measure is the number of people living in households below 60 per cent of median income. A relative approach is essential and this measure is the most widely recognised international poverty threshold. Many people would argue for, and many countries do use, a more complex definition which reflects the multidimensional and dynamic nature of poverty. While such a set of indicators is still very useful, a single and simple headline measure to which politicians and the public can relate is clearly needed. The limitation of the 60 per cent median figure comes in its lack of appeal to the public. Unfortunately, '60 per cent of median income' means little to the man (or woman or child) on the street. Much more meaningful is the approach taken in the JRF's own survey on tackling disadvantage which reveals how many people are unable to afford items that the majority of the public say are necessary and believe that people in Britain should not have to do without.

We have also suggested previously the need for a social justice metric to be measured over time, which would set out a small number of headline indicators illustrating the levels of both deprivation and inequality.

Redistributive taxation

Tackling disadvantage is thankfully honest about the need to consider raising taxes and enhancing redistribution of revenues, while pointing out that the actual level will depend on how many more people move into work and whether those in low paid work become more productive and better paid.

The 2002 Budget did mark a turning point in the government's approach to taxation. Until this point, there had been extreme reticence in admitting the need to raise taxes in order to provide better public services. Labour came to power claiming it had shed its image of 'tax and spend'. The Chancellor chose to increase national insurance rather than income tax to soften the blow in people's perceptions, but in reality it makes little difference to the money in people's pockets. While this departure is encouraging, the link that has been made in the minds of the public is between tax increases and improved public services, particularly the NHS. The link has not been made between tax increases and benefit increases and other poverty reduction policies. This is a challenge – not least because the pattern of spending necessary to deliver the key outcomes that we may wish to prioritise may not match what the electorate appears to want. A contribution to improving health outcomes in the UK might be secured as much by spending more on housing and benefits than spending more money on the NHS.

We would agree with the study that there are some grounds for being optimistic. The annual *British Social Attitudes* survey consistently reveals that a large majority of people support increased spending on 'health, education and social benefits', even if this means higher taxes. The past few years have shown that it is politically possible to give disproportionately more to the less well-off, although, as we have discussed, it is questionable whether people know this has happened. It is also true that we remain a relatively low taxed country. That it is affordable is not really in question, but rather whether it is politically feasible to raise taxes to further progressive ends. A key finding of the Fabian Tax Commission's work on public attitudes[7] was the sense of 'disconnection' people felt between the taxes they pay and the services the taxes pay for. People did not know where their money was going and did not trust the government to spend it wisely. The Tax Commission made two broad recommendations for how a 'reconnection' might be achieved: better information and hypothecation (committing a tax revenue stream directly to a specific spending priority). An open discussion of tax must be central to any debate about the scope for alleviating poverty and disadvantage. Taxation could be made far more fair and progressive, but we are still a very long way in the public debate from perceptions that would allow a progressive reform of inheritance tax or taxation of housing wealth, and for this not to be anything other than political suicide.

Overall, this adds up to the need for two key policy drives. The first is to develop a strategy that illustrates to the public the impact of poverty on individuals and society as a whole and garners their support. The second is to have a more open and honest debate about tax and to further the linking of tax and spending in the minds of the public.

Redesigning the welfare contract
A broken contract

We cannot stop here. A second priority for action must be a comprehensive redesigning of the welfare contract. Once, the welfare system was firmly defined by the insurance principle and benefits were paid according to contributions made. In recognition that this no longer is true, there has been much rhetoric around 'new contracts' and 'new deals'. The demise of the contributory principle in particular has left many people, especially pensioners, feeling that the original contract has been broken and that despite a lifetime's contributions, they are required to live off means-tested benefits. For many others, confusion reigns, with people having little idea of any connection between what they pay in and what they get out, and little idea of what their rights and responsibilities are.

Positive conceptualisation of rights and responsibilities

Why does this matter? A clear understanding between the public and the state is needed to garner the much-needed support for the welfare state but also to enable all individuals to be secure, empowered, active citizens. The primacy of the contributory principle has been overtaken by the concept of 'conditionality' – that receipt of benefits is dependent on individuals fulfilling certain conditions. This is not new but has taken on a different character in recent years. Receipt of unemployment benefits or Jobseeker's Allowance has required individuals to be actively seeking work. Current plans to make Housing Benefit conditional on 'social behaviour', or rather the removal of Housing Benefit if tenants consistently embark on anti-social behaviour, is taking the welfare state in a new direction. Ideas relating to reducing the Child Benefit of parents whose children truant from school have also been mooted.

We are now seeing the role of the welfare system being stretched to shape society in new ways. The welfare system is being asked to go beyond poverty alleviation or promoting opportunities to achieve other outcomes. It would seem we are moving in the direction of perceiving welfare payments not as a right for those who are perceived to have a need but also a way to reinforce certain standards or behaviour in society. New Labour was elected with no obvious social security plan and an instruction for the new Minister for Welfare Reform to 'think the unthinkable'. Frank Field's own views about the inherent superiority of a modernised social insurance system over means testing were rejected by HM Treasury, which was not convinced that the figures added up. But it is perhaps surprising that the contributory principle has been allowed to erode under the current government given its commitment to moving away from a 'something for nothing society'. In some ways contributory benefits embody the notion of a 'something for something society'. With the likely continued fall in the relative value of the basic state pension in future years – at least under a Labour rather than a Conservative government – and the rise in the number of pensioners who are entitled to means-tested benefits (over half of pensioners will be entitled to a pension credit), the contributory principle looks set to weaken further.

We would urge that a *positive conceptualisation* of rights and responsibilities is needed to replace the muddy waters left by the demise of the contributory principle. This does not mean a system whereby benefits are used as penalties, but rather one in which rights are maintained and individuals are given the necessary support and advice to fulfil certain duties or responsibilities. Evidence from the US, where the notion of enhanced conditionality has been implemented in certain states, reveals that outcomes are only positive if the necessary support systems are in place that help people to fulfil their responsibilities. The new approach could be structured around the notion of participation rather than contribution records. For example, John Hills has recently argued that the current pensions system could be developed into a more transparent system that would guarantee a total state pension at a fixed percentage of average earnings for those meeting a participation test, rather than being based on contribution records.[8]

The failure of complexity

In rethinking the relationship between the state and the individual, it feels as if it should go without saying that the relationship must be one that the public can understand. But it doesn't. One of the reasons we have a lack of public support, and indeed a crisis in public confidence in the areas of pensions and long-term care, is that the system is so complex that public understanding is nigh impossible. We have argued elsewhere that simplification must be a first order priority, not as is often the case an add-on or not considered at all.[9] It is encouraging that the Conservatives have accepted this logic and dispiriting that the Labour government remains committed to an overly complex, ill-understood pensions system.

This complexity is often caused by the interaction between state and private resources, with means testing often the key culprit. There are a number of reasons for being concerned about excessive means testing which we explore in the next section, but complexity is a major concern. It is one factor that can lead to the low take-up of some benefits. Complexity often means that people do not claim the benefits to which they are entitled, and this is where complexity manifests itself in poverty. About 1.5 million children live in households with less than 60 per cent of the median income that are not receiving either Income

Support or tax credits.[10] In general, in designing welfare policy we have to stop thinking like Treasury officials or economists and start thinking like benefit recipients. Or rather Treasury officials have to start thinking like benefits recipients in designing welfare policy.

Balancing universalism and targeting

We need to be very clear about one of the central tensions in welfare policy: the balance between universal and targeted policies and their respective roles in alleviating poverty. There is not the space to have a full debate on this here, but it is worth being very clear of the risks inherent in the current shift to greater means testing. *Tackling disadvantage* recognises these and describes the potential stigma, disincentives and lack of take-up that blight a heavily means-tested approach. The report goes on to suggest that a balance is needed between income-contingent benefits and a stable structure of broad entitlements. This could be said to be consistent with the *progressive universalist* approach adopted by the current government. Where the government has gone wrong is through applying progressive universalism to many different individual aspects of the welfare system, rather than looking at how best to achieve a progressive outcome overall. This means individuals and families are often being means tested several times at any one time, and then persistently across their lifetime. To have a progressive outcome you don't need to be progressive at every stage and with every policy. This adds up to a very confused picture of support, with people – and, one suspects, policy makers – unable to understand the overall pattern of incentives implicit in the system. There is scope to be more imaginative about the progressive universalist approach, in a way which maintains broad support and does not engender dependency, or penalise effort or thrift.

Social housing is an interesting example here. Households have to illustrate 'priority need' to gain access to a social tenancy and then they have a right to permanent help for the future. By offering lifetime tenancies, are we encouraging dependency? The alternative is to make tenancies short-term and the continuation of a tenancy subject to some form of means test. But this in itself can encourage individuals to maintain their failure to provide for themselves (for fear of losing their home). There is no easy answer. Incentives to make people provide for themselves perhaps offer a better route. Access to incapacity benefits reveals a similar quandary. Individuals must prove their incapacity and continue to prove their incapacity in order to receive benefits, but must prove their capacity to work in order to receive work opportunities. The Government should take more seriously the fear disabled people may have of losing benefit: any review of incapacity benefits should be frozen for a fixed period of job search activity.

Empowering individuals across the life cycle

Education is central to the ability of individuals to become empowered citizens, but for reasons of space we do not discuss education here, despite IPPR's work in this area.[11]

An early start

Tackling disadvantage recognises that services are needed to support families if we are to tackle disadvantage. This has been central to IPPR's work on the early years of life. By the time a child reaches its first birthday, much of the foundation for the rest of life will be laid.[12] This first year and indeed pregnancy are critical to the well-being and life chances of every child.

As *Tackling disadvantage* describes, there is a careful balance to be found between providing legitimate support for parents and avoiding excessive intervention in the family, often viewed as the private sphere of people's lives. The profound impact that the parent–child relationship has on an infant's development has been neglected in public policy. We think government must get more involved in these early years if a significant difference is to be made in tackling poverty and disadvantage in the long term. This means better provision of social and emotional support for parents through transforming the health visiting and midwifery roles. It also means looking at the adequacy of social security support for the under-25s. Evidence that financial support during pregnancy can lead to better child outcomes provides a compelling case for its introduction.

Continuity for young people

Providing support in the early years of a child's life is vital, but it is not an alternative to providing support and provision when they are older, in their early and late teens. Evidence shows that early interventions maintain their impact on a young person's life chances only if they are sustained and built upon. New initiatives, such as *Connexions*, children's centres and positive activities for young people are under way, but there is still a long way to go and many gaps to be plugged. A key concern is that services for young people can lack continuity. Young people themselves tend not to think that they have something to rely on. Young people's hopes and ambitions are raised by the provision of activities and services at one moment, only to be dampened when funding runs out, services are remodelled or discontinued, or staffing problems emerge.

There is a real challenge in developing a framework that allows services for young people to engage with them over a period of time and maintain their trust and interest with new models that integrate their services, using the *Sure Start* experience as a guide. A type of 'Sure Futures' model[13] could emerge which would combine health, social care, education and sport and arts activities for teenagers, potentially with parental support built in.

Assets to protect and empower

While a good start in life is highly desirable given its particularly strong impact on later well-being, individuals need to be secure and empowered throughout their lifetimes. The recent interest in asset-based welfare has been born from recognition that assets provide security in times of change and also empower people to take opportunities to improve their lives. The Government is introducing a Child Trust Fund for all newborn babies which will mean all young adults will have access to assets on turning 18. Pilots of the Saving Gateway are also under way which offer matched incentives to people in low-income communities.

Evidence from the US shows that the power of this approach comes not only from availability of resources but also from the psychological impact that asset holding can bestow. The process of asset building can connect people who own nothing and have limited opportunities to a future where more might be possible. We would advocate an extension of these ideas[14] and the development of a second generation of asset-based policies. This might include strategic use of grants in the benefit system to help people cope with unpredictable events, or policies that help social housing tenants to accumulate assets (through more extensive availability of the Joseph Rowntree Housing Trust's New Earswick model of flexible shared ownership or other equity stake ideas).

Conclusion

We must choose to tackle disadvantage and this means developing a strategy which garners the support of the public. It needs to illustrate over time the impact and consequences of poverty and disadvantage and to start to link in people's minds the taxes they pay with the type of society we want to live in. Galvanising public support will become less of a challenge if the welfare contract is redesigned. This is not a new grand plan but a clear articulation of rights and responsibilities, thus removing us from the limbo of the demise of the contributory principle and the muddy waters of current complexity. There is scope to be imaginative and more strategic about a progressive universalist approach.

Further resources will be needed to sustain and enhance existing policies but more is needed. New approaches and ideas are still required. These could include:

- extra support in the early years of life (and during pregnancy), given the importance of this period for later life chances, including the offer of social and emotional support for parents;
- new types of service to engage with young people over a period of time and maintain their trust and interest, and a 'Sure Futures' model which could combine health, social care, education and sport and arts activities for teenagers, potentially with parental support built in;
- further policies which help build up people's assets to provide security in times of change and empower people to take opportunities to improve their lives.

These ideas, together with the proposals in *Tackling disadvantage*, could mean that we are able to build a society in which no one suffers poverty and disadvantage – an ambition that we all surely have to pursue with urgency and vigour.

Notes

1   Joseph Rowntree Foundation, *Inquiry into income and wealth*, JRF, 1996, Vol. 1, and Vol. 2 (by John Hills).

2   P. Robinson, *Time to choose justice*, IPPR, 2001.

3   J. Adams, P. Robinson and A. Vigor, *A new regional policy for the UK*, IPPR, 2003.

4   S. Regan and K. Stanley, *The mission million*, IPPR, 2003.

5   R. Lister, 'Doing good by stealth: The politics of poverty and inequality under New Labour', *New Economy*, June 2001.

6   G. Holtham, 'Comment: Poverty targets and reports', in C. Oppenheim (ed.) *An inclusive society: Strategies for tackling poverty*, IPPR, 1998.

7   The Commission on Taxation and Citizenship, *Paying for progress: A new politics of tax for public spending*, The Fabian Society, 2000.

8   J. Hills, *Inclusion or insurance? National Insurance and the future of the contributory principle*, CASE paper 68, London School of Economics, 2003.

9   R. Brooks, S. Regan and P. Robinson, *A new contract for retirement*, IPPR, 2001.

10   M. Brewer, T. Clark and A. Goodman, *The Government's child poverty target: How much progress has been made?* IFS, 2002.

11   J. Hallgarten, *School league tables: Have they outlived their usefulness?* IPPR, 2001; W. Piatt and P. Robinson, *Opportunity for whom? Options for funding and structure of post-16 education*, IPPR 2001.

12   L. Harker and L. Kendall, *An equal start*, IPPR, 2003.

13   L. Edwards and B. Hatch, *Passing time: A report about young people and communities*, IPPR, 2003.

14   W. Paxton (ed.) *Equal shares?* IPPR, 2003.

2 | Labour's unfinished business

Roger Wicks, Social Market Foundation

The Government's social policy programme has made significant progress since 1997. Central objectives, such as tackling disadvantage, child poverty in particular, based on important, fresh analysis, have been set and pursued with rigour by numerous policy initiatives. Critically, they have been supported with significant extra spending. The Joseph Rowntree Foundation report, *Tackling disadvantage: A 20-year enterprise*,[1] however, is a timely reminder of the colossal work in hand.

The new fiscal welfare state

A strategy aimed at tackling disadvantage will inevitably balance targeted, or means-tested, welfare with universal provision. All governments since 1945 have managed and developed a mixed economy of universal and means-tested welfare. There have been striking variations: the development of universal provision by Labour, for example the move to a universal Child Benefit in 1975; and the sharp focus on means-tested benefits, with diminishing value, in the 1980s. Since 1997, there has been as much continuity as change. The focus on means testing for families (Child Tax Credit) and the elderly (the Pension Credit) is unprecedented by Labour in office.[2] However, Child Benefit has greatly increased in value from 1998. It is, more accurately, the social insurance system that has been most affected.[3] Nevertheless the history of social policy research has been dominated by the polarised pro-targeting and pro-universal camps dichotomy.[4]

Yet, in reality, both have always existed and should continue to do so. Housing Benefit for example should never be available to middle-class homeowners. Any welfare state will always provide, as a minimum, a safety net whose primary assumption is to support those in need. Such an assessment inevitably demands some kind of test of means which will require citizens to present information proving their position. This can be administered in a harsh or accommodating, complicated or simple way; but there will always be a form of targeting with its associated problems, critically the issue of take-up.[5] A succession of governments since World War Two essentially reinvented the means test with the primary hope of increasing take-up.[6]

The JRF sets as its first principle, 'to increase the capacity of poorer households', and the report argues for giving 'systematic priority to the disadvantaged'.[7] In practical terms this means endeavouring to make sure that, 20 years from now, 'as few people as possible live on incomes below 60 per cent of the median'. However, the report goes on to warn against the trend towards means testing[8] and summarises some of the well-documented problems: the poverty trap, saving disincentives, and take-up. Critically, there is no understanding that means testing can equal redistribution. The redistribution that has occurred since 1997 (or, more accurately, 1998)[9] is due to increases in Income Support and Working Families Tax Credit,[10] as well as Child Benefit.

In short, means testing is a wholly different policy tool in the hands of a centre-left government compared to a centre-right one. While a centre-right government's means-testing methodology aims to secure a safety net welfare state (often falling foul of the classic dictum of the eminent social policy thinker Richard Titmuss that 'services for the poor are invariably poor services'), with reduced levels of provision, Labour's is tied to a strategy of redistribution – rarely voiced, but redistribution nevertheless. The report fails to recognise New Labour's distinctive approach to welfare which has recast the classic means-testing versus universalist debate: the so-called 'progressive universalism'[11] of the Child Tax Credit for which 80 per cent of families are eligible, with the poorest receiving a far higher award, banishing the historical problem of stigma.

Richard Titmuss used to decry what he saw as a hidden 'fiscal welfare state': a system of tax allowances and perks for the middle class. New Labour's increasing integration of the tax and benefits system for the poor, and attendant redistribution, may yet come to be seen as a new fiscal welfare state for social democracy.

Child poverty: Do the tools serve the target?

In his William Beveridge commemoration lecture of March 1999, the Prime Minister pledged to eradicate child poverty in 20 years, halve it in ten and cut it by a quarter by 2004–5. The overall and midway targets are extremely unlikely to be met. The Government managed only half of the 1 million children it promised to take out of poverty during its first term. The number of children living below the poverty line[12] fell from 4.2 million in 1998–9 to 3.8 million in 2001–2. So there will need to be fewer than 3.1 million children in poverty in 2004–5 to meet the first target. What are the implications here for the Government's chosen strategy? Are they the wrong policies? Or, if they are the correct policies, do they have to be extended? This paper supports a programme based on the third suggestion.

Labour's strategy is threefold and represents a huge programme of extra spending: strengthening the value of work by introducing and increasing tax credits; encouraging the transition from welfare to work with the New Deal and investment in child care; and increasing universal Child Benefit. All three need to be accelerated if the targets are to be met and this requires substantial further investment over the long term.

As a programme for immediate action, an increase in the basic rate of income tax by 1p would raise £2.8 billion; an equivalent rise in National Insurance would raise £3 billion.[13] Either is now essential, specifically earmarked for the child poverty programme. The extra funds should primarily increase the value of the Child Tax Credit and support a new second phase of welfare to work, but also the Social Fund (discussed below). Such a programme is particularly necessary if families who live further below the poverty line are to be targeted. The perennial poverty paradox is that it is easier for those closest to the defined poverty line to be brought above it rather than those, largely workless, family households who are further down.[14]

The Institute for Fiscal Studies has estimated that at current planned benefit/credit levels, child poverty is likely to fall to 3.3 million children in 2004/05,[15] 200,000 short of the government's 3.1 million target. To reach this level, the child element of the Child Tax Credit would need to be increased by a mere £3 a week, costing £1 billion. With a 1 per cent increase to direct taxation, however, government could afford to go further. To increase the child element by £5 a week would take 400,000 children above the poverty line and would cost a further £0.7 billion, a total £1.7 billion.[16]

The public support for the 1 per cent increase in National Insurance in April 2002 was central to the progress of the current government's public policy. The Government went on the offensive, arguing that the future of the NHS depended on greater revenues generated through higher taxation.[17] If the case for extra spending can be made for the NHS why not for child poverty? The effects of the NI increase is unclear to many of the public; much of the extra money has rightly been channelled into extra pay in the health sector, but the tangible value to health outcomes is a medium- to long-term enterprise. The consequences of extra spending on social security/tax credits would, by contrast, be clear and immediate. However, ministers would need to be more forthright about their redistribution. The End Child Poverty Coalition,[18] and the support it receives from government, is an important development but it requires government to be as forthright about the means as it is about the all-important end.

Larger families

Are the Government's policy tools appropriate, however, to reduce child poverty in large families? This is a neglected issue[19] which requires a radical reorientation of welfare provision. Almost one in four children (23 per cent) are in three-child households and 11 per cent live in households with four or more children.[20] There is no doubt that children in large families have a greater risk of living in poverty. Children in families with three or more children represent half of all poor children, and the chances of being poor in a four-child family are twice as high as in a one- or two-child family.[21]

On the one hand lone parents and young mothers have a higher risk of poverty and they are all also more likely to represent smaller families. On the other hand, some ethnic groups have high rates of unemployment and they are also more likely to have larger families. There is a marked lack of detailed social policy analysis on large families and child poverty levels.

According to Jonathan Bradshaw, this issue strikes right at the heart of the principle of equity which demands 'that a child should not be poor because of its birth order'. He argues:

> However in a distributional system entirely determined by the labour market, larger families are more likely to be poor, because earnings are not adjusted by the number of people dependent

43

Table 2.1 Poverty rate and proportion of children in poverty by family size

Number of children in family	Poverty rate (%)	% of children poor	All (%)
One	24	18	23
Two	25	35	43
Three	36	27	23
Four or more	56	20	11
All	31	100	100

Source: Department for Work and Pensions, 2002
Note: Rate and proportion relate to families with equivalent income less than 60 per cent of the median after housing costs, and including the self-employed.

on them (except in Japan). It is partly for this reason that welfare states in the industrial world intervene with a package of tax benefits, cash benefits, reductions in charges and direct services which together assist parents with the costs of child rearing. To what extent do our arrangements in Britain meet the equity principle that a child should not be poor because of its birth order? [22]

The short answer to the Bradshaw test is that they do not. The Child Tax Credit is worth £27.75 per child per week for families earning up to £13,000 (it is withdrawn by 37p for every pound above a threshold). In 2003–4 Child Benefit for the eldest or only child is worth £16.05 per week; and for each additional child, £10.75 each week. An attempt to pay families more for their additional children would require significant extra resources. If not, it presents a paradox, as Bradshaw observes: 'Given no extra revenue, if one were to shift the tax/benefit system in favour of large families there is a danger of reducing child poverty less for large families than you increase it for small families (because there are more of them).'[23]

There are possible policy solutions from abroad. In the state of Wisconsin in the US a larger credit is offered to families with three or more children. (At the federal level and in every other state the amount of Earned Income Tax Credit available to families with three or more children is the same as that available for those with two children.) What has been the impact of the Wisconsin move and would a similar approach work in the UK? There is an urgent need for research here.

There is a critical political, as well as policy, tension with which ministers need to grapple. Current benefit/credit priorities threaten Labour's child poverty targets, yet policies which seek to encourage 'the poor' to have more children (à la council house placement prioritisation) would be heavily criticised by the political right.

Welfare and indebtedness – the need to recast the safety net

The growing level of indebtedness presents a new challenge to social policy. Policy has not evolved to meet what is a critical new social problem. The welfare state's basic function is to support people and their dependants in times of need. There are typically further objectives: redistribution down the income scale and over the life cycle; extra support to meet the cost of raising children; and, a relatively recent innovation, to support people in low-income jobs through tax credits. However, the so called 'safety net' exists to protect against hardships which often follow unemployment or long periods of illness. It is also an objective which receives broader support across the political spectrum.[24] The current government's analysis[25] of over-indebtedness is a sound one. Ministers wisely distinguish between manageable, indeed desirable, life-chances transforming *debt* and debilitating *over-indebtedness* which can prove catastrophic for the individual and his or her family. The remedies, however, have not followed.

Yet the issue of indebtedness, and its fluid relationship with poverty, demands a new response with a reformed Social Fund at its heart.[26] The current system is an antiquated part of the welfare state that fails to address the modern realities of poverty and indebtedness. The system of loans which are repaid through Income Support deductions contradicts government social policy strategy by both exacerbating the dependency culture and keeping households in poverty. The Social Fund should be both reformed and more generously funded.[27] The aim would be both to support the indebted and to stop those on the brink of indebtedness borrowing unwisely. Budgeting loans are only available for people receiving income-related benefits such as Income Support. Such a framework is unsuited to the realities of debt: many people on the brink of over-indebtedness, such as those in low-paid work or in irregular work, are not supported. The Fund should also be restructured and extended to support those on low incomes. A sudden loss of income can create over-indebtedness, yet people moving on to Income Support, or another qualifying benefit, are ineligible for the first six months.

The Social Fund must be more widely publicised so as to deter people from taking inappropriate loans; periodically, correspondence from the state to the citizen (Inland Revenue, Jobcentre Plus) should include clear information about the scheme. However, the loans would need to be more generous.[28] Three distinct sets of people are currently being failed by the system. First, people use the fund alongside other forms of credit,[29] which a better funded system could prevent. A second group of potential claimants are refused help where demand outstrips capacity. Third, the 'double debt' rule[30] must be abolished as, again, it fails to take into account the realities of the relationship between poverty and indebtedness.

Long-term policy strategy, however, is being put in place and financial education is, rightly, critical. Improving the financial literacy and numeracy of consumers is a key government objective.

The poverty trap

The Government's attempt to combat poverty and increase work incentives centres on overcoming the poverty trap. The poverty trap closes when somebody starts to pay Income Tax and National Insurance contributions at the same time as their benefit or tax credit entitlement is withdrawn, resulting in a minimal increase to net income and destroying the incentive to find a better paid job or to work longer hours. Labour's approach since 1997 has been to 'make work pay' by introducing in-work benefits, or tax credits, as well as a minimum wage. There has been considerable progress, although a tax credits regime, like any other form of means testing, will never overcome the poverty trap entirely. Tax credits attempt to negate this problem via a taper: a rate at which the value of the credit is slowly withdrawn.[31] The taper aims to blunt the bite of the poverty trap, but the nature of the beast is and will remain a disincentive. The rate will always have to taper out if it is to target a particular income range, distinguishing it from a universal benefit.

What has been lacking in this largely progressive strategy is an analysis of the role played by Housing Benefit, both as an effective form of provision in itself[32] and in contributing to increasing living standards by encouraging work.

A failure to address Housing Benefit reform means that Labour has, to a great extent, tackled the unemployment trap (which strikes when the value of unemployment benefit puts people off taking low-income work), but not the poverty trap. It is easy to see how a regime which removes the subsidised payment of rent at a stroke when the claimant finds work would disincentivise a move into paid work.[33]

Housing tax credit

There is clear case now for a new housing tax credit which would both reform the present inefficient and expensive Housing Benefit system and serve to improve work incentives. It would work together with a new Income Support system that included a new housing component, for those out of work and retired. It would be relatively straightforward to extend a housing tax credit to low-income households in work. Critically, it should be available to tenants and owner-occupiers alike. Figures which show that 50 per cent of those living in poverty are homeowners highlight the problem with the current regime where 92 per cent of state provision goes to tenants.[34] It could either be available for all those who claim it who currently receive the Working Tax Credit, or form a component part of the WTC. A recent report argued that it 'would be relatively simple to administer, as well as effective in reducing the maximum amount of benefit that recipients could lose at the margins as their earnings increased'.[35]

One disadvantage of a credit, but not one which outweighs the benefits, is that, like the Child Tax Credit, a larger number of people would be subject to a means test. This potentially represents a new trap further up the income scale. Better, however, a trap high up the scale, where the marginal impact of every extra pound is less, than at the bottom where every pound really counts. At the bottom end, the minimum wage (now £4.50 an hour) and the new in-work tax credits have put down a floor that ensures that work should be more profitable than benefits.

Depending on the gradient of the taper (the rate at

which the credit is withdrawn up the income scale), the new credit may well increase the cost of housing provision (compared to Housing Benefit), because HB is not available to homeowners in work,[36] although there should be huge savings from a decline in the levels of fraud.

Current government strategy is to move towards a system, currently piloted, of a move to a cash-in-hand benefit (HB goes straight to landlords) in order to empower citizens. This is a welcome move away from a paternalistic welfare state: imagine a child benefit regime in which state officials chose which goods were to be bought with the weekly benefit. A credit would not dilute this idea.

As Peter Kemp has proposed, there would also need to be different levels of credit for those in different parts of the country, since rents vary enormously.[37] It would probably need to be pegged to the average local rent rather than the national or even regional average. This is the greatest drawback to the proposal. The complications involved would be real and potentially severe, particularly if the new social administrator that is the Inland Revenue does not learn from the problems associated with the introduction of the Child Tax Credit in 2003.

Employment: What next for welfare to work?

Welfare to work is the social policy ministers have the least trouble trumpeting, and deservedly so. There is a clear political narrative and the policy has bedded down well: encouraging the unemployed to take work with both carrots and sticks – improved work-focused training and benefit sanctions, respectively. Welfare to work has also been given institutional expression: the Department for Work and Pensions incorporated the DSS and employment side of the DfEE. The Benefits Agency, which pays out benefits, and the Employment Service, where jobless people search for vacancies, have been merged into Jobcentre Plus.

It is hard to say how many of the jobs created by the New Deal – which in total has cost more than £1.7 billion – would have been created regardless of positive economic climes. It is, however, true that long-term youth unemployment is now at the historically low level of 36,000. There remain, however, critical issues in employment policy and it is alarming that welfare to work has not been developed in these directions. Energy seems to have dissipated from the huge welfare to work momentum in the 1997–2001 parliamentary term.

There are three distinct contemporary problems. Firstly, there are currently 1 million unemployed people claiming benefits and this figure has stayed at around this level since 1999. There is a specific demographic problem with those from the age of 50 up to pensionable age. Secondly, a large proportion of this number have employability issues, either a lack of basic skills or more acute social problems. Thirdly, large areas of the country have employment shortages which make redundant the welfare to work dynamic.

There are three distinct tasks which are generated by this analysis. The first, crucial, imperative is to create a permanent New Deal, sticks and carrots included, for all long-term jobless. Except for lone parents and the disabled, who have their own New Deal schemes, all new claimants who remain on benefits for six months should enter the New Deal 'gateway'. The second is for a rigorous basic skills programme which builds on the current Basic Skills pilots. The third is an extension of the *StepUp* programme which extends the New Deal's reach by supporting employers in less prosperous areas of the UK. In many ways the two programmes represent the genesis of a more rigorous second phase of welfare to work reform. These receive little wider comment, and strangely no great trumpeting by ministers. Yet they represent a radical proposition in employment policy. More importantly, they represent the seeds of the future of welfare to work.

There are considerable drawbacks to Labour's 'supply side' focus in social and economic policy. If employment rates fall, how will welfare to work work? Under the current, highly favourable economic conditions, unemployment benefit recipients may be effectively encouraged to look for jobs; but unless the jobs are available, the system fails. The impact of the New Deal has been regionally patchy due to differing economic conditions. The New Deal 'works best where it is needed least', according to Ron Martin.[38] He argues that the first proper study of the scheme's effectiveness has shown that in the South (but not London) the New Deal has worked reasonably well: 'it is working quite well in the South, where unemployment is already low and where almost all the new jobs are being created. But in the North, no matter how employable you make people, if jobs aren't there they won't get them.' There are also wide differences in how long people remain employed. Six months after leaving the New Deal for a job, as few as 10 per cent of people are still employed in the least advantaged areas. In the best areas about 50 per cent were still in work.[39]

Should the state play a more direct role in creating work? This would seem to be off the New Labour radar but the Department for Work and Pensions is currently piloting a programme in StepUp which directly pays employers the full cost of the unemployed worker. But should not a credible rights and responsibilities agenda also bring duties to the state? The concept of 'mutual obligation' has been taken on board by the Australian government, who recognise that their part of the bargain is to stimulate economic growth so that jobs are available for the unemployed to get.

The StepUp scheme was introduced to plug the gap in demand. It provides the jobless with work, paying employers the full cost of taking someone on. It guarantees participants a full-time job at the national minimum wage for up to 50 weeks, and gives them personalised support. It is largely based on Richard Layard's strong argument, aimed at cutting benefit dependency and the cycle of deprivation by doing 'something dramatic to break with the past'.[40] A cross between the Intermediate Labour Market (ILM) and subsidised employment, StepUp provides a guaranteed full-time job on at least the minimum wage, for up to 50 weeks. Participants are given the same employment rights and in-work benefits as other employees and a 33-hour week in the local labour market. Importantly, the new jobs cannot displace other workers. A StepUp participant is given a choice of jobs, but cannot refuse all of them without good reason, otherwise benefits are sanctioned (in the same way as they already are under the main New Deal for Young People). The Joseph Rowntree Foundation evaluated ILMs in 2000 and was very positive, finding they worked much better in getting people back into employment than other schemes.[41]

It is striking that the StepUp programme, which represents a demand-led approach to employment, has received almost no media comment. There is room for a greater extension of this programme too. It is difficult to judge in which areas such investment is most required. There would need to be coordination with local authorities and Regional Development Agencies, as well as with any new regional government structures.

The Basic Skills pilots oblige people lacking basic skills to attend free further education courses or lose benefit. Pilots were set up in 2001 to test different methods of raising the basic skills of unemployed people, to complement the government's basic skills strategy (*Skills for life*)[42] of improving the numeracy and literacy of 750,000 people in the next two years. It is estimated one in three of the long-term unemployed have a basic skills deficiency. Jobseekers aged between 25 and 49 who have been claiming benefits for at least six months will have their basic literacy and numeracy skills assessed. If they need literacy and numeracy skills training, and it is appropriate for them (this was added to the final draft of the regulation, to ensure people who cannot go through mainstream skills courses are not unfairly sanctioned), they must go on a course. Those who refuse will lose their Jobseeker's Allowance for two weeks. If they refuse to participate again in the following 12 months they will lose four weeks' Jobseeker's Allowance.[43]

The basic skills initiative should be rolled out nationally. Responsibility is key: the state must ensure that courses are of a high quality and freely available.

Assets – the forgotten redistribution

Left-of-centre governments in Europe have traditionally focused, and rightly so, on the distribution of income. A key component of the social democratic settlement of the postwar years in the UK can be summarised as a strategy to improve the living standards of the poorest by creating a framework of benefits which redistribute income via progressive taxation. This strategy ignored an analysis of the distribution of capital, or assets. In periods of widespread absolute poverty the redistribution of income will always be the priority and it will continue to be central to social democratic reform, particularly when aimed at supporting families with children. However, the empowerment and social inclusion of poorer families requires a broader spread of assets, such as savings.

The ownership of assets in the UK is unequal, being heavily polarised between the assetless and the wealthy. The share of marketable wealth of the top 50 per cent rose from 91 per cent to 94 per cent between 1982 and 1999,[44] while the number of households owning no assets doubled over the same period.[45] It is the result of this inequality that is most important: the impact on life chances. There are clear correlations between the holding of assets and time spent in employment and general good health.[46]

Income-based benefits alone should enable people to live in dignity while out of work, but they will not be enough to enable people to take control of their destinies (and neither will incomes in the lower ranges be enough, even with a generous extension of tax credits). Means-tested social security benefits sustain in periods of hardship; but a spread of assets should transform the lives of many. A new distribution of assets, and resultant redistribution, would provide a new policy tool in the strategy to tackle poverty.

The proposed Child Trust Funds represent an important, though tentative, beginning, but they can go much further. At the age of 18 individuals should be presented with a grant which should be first, substantial, second, conditional and, third, universal. This paper will not offer a precise amount but the fund should be in the region of £10,000 for the poorest, £5,000 for the more wealthy. It is vital that the application of the grant is prescribed: education, training or an investment either into an asset or a business venture. There is a strong libertarian case which argues that a conditional sum would be but a further application of the paternalist welfare state.[47] There is force to such a critique, but there are two arguments for defining the grant's application. It is easy to envisage the more infantile components of the British media illustrating the abuse of the money by young people on receipt. The effect would be to undermine the scheme and arm any future centre-right government with a popular reason to abolish the grants. More critically, however, a welfare state based on rights *and* responsibilities is entitled to ensure that grants which are paid for by taxpayers (who for at least a generation, of course, would not themselves have benefited from the policy) are used broadly for investment.

Progressive and universal

It is important now that any development of asset-based welfare is a universal one, available to all young people regardless of their or their family's income. At the same time, as indicated above, a larger grant should go to the poorest; perhaps those on the Working Tax Credit and Income Support. The main reason why the fund should also be universal is that there is no current provision of this kind. It would make it both fair (the grant is equal) and sustainable (galvanising middle class political clout). If Gordon Brown's conception of progressive universalism in welfare is to move beyond tax credits, this could be the way.

Only one piece of the package

The new funds represent the seeds of a much greater overhaul of social provision in the UK than anything since the establishment of universal provision of education and health services in the 1940s. There is, however, a danger of pitching the policy as panacea.

Since the rise of thinking on asset-based welfare in the 1990s, debate has broadly fallen into two camps,[48] between those presenting it as a panacea and those fundamentally opposed. Both sides are wrong and right, and their mistake is to polarise their own positions. The distribution of assets, and need for their redistribution, has been argued here, but it represents only one part of a broader strategy. For undoubtedly there are large numbers who barely subsist in absolute poverty who are in no position to save.

The data on absolute poverty are at least as hazy and as controversial as the definition of relative poverty, but the 1997 Breadline Britain survey estimated that over 2 million children go without two or more items, such as a properly fitting pair of shoes or a warm home.[49] One response here is to dismiss the issue of assets out of hand. Martin Barnes has argued that 'it is simply income poverty which means the poor are unable to save; this begs the question as to whether a more appropriate policy response is simply to increase incomes.'[50] This response is rejected here, but is illustrated as an important note of caution.

The distribution of capital has been long ignored by the centre-left and these tentative early moves to redress the balance are welcome – though the sums offered are very small – but it is no panacea and ideally forms a critical part of a programme which must include many of the other policies raised here.

Conclusion

Labour planned to 'think the unthinkable' on welfare when the party came to office in 1997. In many respects Labour has thought and done the unthinkable, with tackling poverty and disadvantage a central theme. Social policy has broken new ground and diverges from both its Conservative and Labour government predecessors. In many of the areas discussed here there are important developments – contentious and problematic in many cases, but significant in terms of policy development and implementation. None more so than tax credits, and with this unique transfer of power to the Treasury comes a new bond between social security and employment. The prime implication for the family is that the levels of investment in children are unprecedented. The abolition of child poverty remains Labour's most ambitious social policy objective, but extra spending will still be required. On work, the New Deal is justifiably heralded by ministers for tackling long-term youth unemployment but, as unemployment remains resolutely at the 1 million mark, there are dangers that welfare to work has run out of steam. There are seeds of an important new phase, however, in existing government pilots. Similarly, there is new thinking on the empowering potential of assets, though this is no simple panacea even in the long term.

Despite fresh analysis and novel policy-making, however, there remains what a social democratic government must regard as unfinished business, coupled with a failure to respond to social change. The Social Fund is the main example; a crucial area of policy which requires both extra funding and reorientation. Indebtedness presents a new social ill to which the welfare state is yet to respond. This paper argues, too, that fresh thinking is required to deal with poverty in larger families, with clear implications for the benefits and tax credit system. A similar demographic blind-spot lies in the levels of poverty among homeowners and a Housing Benefit system which misses the mark,

If these issues are not currently seen as policy priorities – and they certainly never headline the political debate – the Labour government is fighting poverty and disadvantage with one hand tied behind its back.

Notes

1   D. Darton, D. Hirsch and J. Strelitz, *Tackling disadvantage: A 20-year enterprise*, JRF, 2003.

2   The Labour governments of the 1960s in fact introduced a range of means-tested benefits, for example the Housing Allowance, which is now Housing Benefit, but the targeted approach was not as central as it is now, neither in terms of spending or numbers subject to it.

3   Since the mid-1960s the most conspicuous development of British social security policy has been the decline of benefits paid directly from individual contributions through National Insurance. This decline became very steep during the Thatcher years and has continued, at a reduced gradient, since 1997. In 1964, 73 per cent of the social security bill was paid out in contributory benefits. By 2003 this had fallen to about 45 per cent. That decline has continued under Labour. Incapacity benefits have been reduced and the eligibility requirements relaxed, the widow's pension is now paid for a year rather than until remarriage, maternity allowances have been extended to mothers without a complete contributions record and the link between entitlement and contributions has been weakened with respect to the second state pension.

4   The current incarnation pitches New Labour's focus on targeting against the Conservative Party and IPPR universalism.

5   J. Bradshaw and A. Deacon, *Reserved for the poor: The means test in British social policy,* Basil Blackwell and Martin Robertson, 1983.

6   National Assistance was changed to Supplementary Benefit under Labour in 1966, then into Income Support by the Thatcher government in 1984 before being reissued by its Tory successor into Jobseeker's Allowance in 1996. Likewise Family Income Supplement became Family Credit which became Working Families Tax Credit in 1999, which in April 2003 was integrated into a new Child Tax Credit (CTC).

7   *Tackling disadvantage*, p. 16.

8   Ibid., pp. 32–3.

9   Institute of Fiscal Studies (IFS), *Green Budget*, IFS, 2003.

10   Along with the Children's Tax Credit, which replaced Married Couple's Allowance, these were both integrated in April 2003 into the Child Tax Credit.

11   P. Collins and R. Wicks, 'On means testing and tax credits', *Prospect*, May 2003.

12   The poverty line is defined as 60 per cent below median income and these figures are calculated after housing costs.

13   IFS, *Green Budget*.

14   See D. Piachaud and H. Sutherland, *Changing poverty post-1997*, CASE paper 63, London School of Economics, 2002, p. 13.

15   M. Brewer and G. Kaplan, 'What do the child poverty targets mean for the child tax credit?', in IFS, *Green Budget*, p. 49. The authors 'assume that the population, employment rates and household composition do not change from their 2000–01 values, but that real earnings grow in line with past trends'.

16   These proposed rises are above any increases in line with earnings growth (included in the public finance forecasts).

17   There has been a discernible shift in thinking on the link between spending and welfare over the course of the Parliament. By way perhaps of forewarning of the first two years which would see Labour adopt the spending plans of the Conservatives, the general election manifesto read: 'The myth that the solution to every problem is increased spending has been comprehensively dispelled... More spending has brought neither greater fairness nor less poverty. Quite the reverse... The level of public spending is no longer the best measure of the effectiveness of government action in the public interest' (Labour election manifesto, 1997). Yet the key areas of social

security policy, pensioners and families and child poverty would later see large increases in expenditure from the 1998 Budget on: 'The Government has increased support for all families with children with the largest ever rise in Child Benefit' (Treasury, Budget, 2000).

18   The coalition brings together a number of poverty and family voluntary groups, was formed in 2001 aiming to monitor and secure the government's child poverty objectives. See www.ecpc.org.uk/.

19   A notable exception is L. Adelman and J. Bradshaw's *Children in poverty in Britain: An analysis of the Family Resources Survey 1994/95* (1998). See also *Characteristics of large families*, Department for Work and Pensions (DWP), April 2003.

20   *Family Resources Survey*, DWP, 2002.

21   *Households Below Average Income*, DWP, 2002.

22   Jonathan Bradshaw, *Child poverty and large families: A research note*, Social Policy Research Unit, University of York, 2002, available at http://www-users.york.ac.uk/~jrb1/.

23   Ibid., p. 5.

24   Even the minimalist conceptions of social policy of the New Right accept the safety net principle.

25   Performance and Innovation Unit (PIU, now Strategy Unit), *Lending support: Modernising the government's use of loans*, March 2002.

26   This discussion tackles the loan, or 'discretionary', aspects of the Social Fund. The Fund has two distinct parts: non-discretionary grants, such as the Sure Start Maternity Grants, Cold Weather Payments and Winter Fuel Payments, linked to specific conditions or life events; and discretionary grants and loans, like Budgeting Loans and Crisis Loans, designed to assist unexpected or occasional costs.

27   The gross discretionary budget for 2003/04 is £677.5 million, of which £519.3 million is estimated to be provided through the repayment of loans.

28   National Association of Citizens Advice Bureaux report, *Unfair and underfunded: CAB evidence on what's wrong with the Social Fund*, October 2002.

29   DSS Research Report no. 125, DSS, 2002.

30   The 'double debt' rule states that people cannot top up loans until they have repaid a substantial amount. All outstanding Budgeting Loan debt is doubled when calculating how much applicants can borrow.

31   The number of people facing very high marginal tax/deduction rates, above 90 per cent, has substantially reduced – from 130,000 in

1997 to 45,000 today.

32 Twenty years ago in 1984, only the second birthday of Housing Benefit, a leader in The Times described it as 'the biggest administrative fiasco in the history of the welfare state'.

33 P. Kemp, *Housing Benefit: Time for reform,* JRF, 1998.

34 R. Burrows, *Poverty and home ownership in contemporary Britain,* JRF/The Policy Press, January 2003.

35 *Housing Benefit reform: Next steps,* by Peter Kemp, Steve Wilcox and David Rhodes, Joseph Rowntree Foundation, 2002.

36 These arguments are set out in Kemp, *Housing Benefit.*

37 Ibid.

38 See www.adset.org.uk/Update99/12-99-06.htm.

39 Ibid.

40 R. Layard, *Welfare to work and the fight against long term unemployment,* DfEE, 2000.

41 'Properly managed, they can deliver better outcomes, in particular, a more sustained progression from welfare to work than other programmes for the long-term unemployed. Although getting long-term unemployed people back into work is the main objective of three-quarters of ILM programmes, many also provide additional local services and therefore contribute to neighbourhood regeneration. Compared with other labour market initiatives for the same target group, ILM programmes offer equivalent or better value for money after adjustments are made for the value of the services provided, the higher job placement and durability of employment rates and the higher incomes gained' (www.jrf.org.uk/knowledge/ findings/socialpolicy/970.asp).

42 See www.dfes.gov.uk/get-on/.

43 As with the New Deal for Young People, hardship payments will be available for those who need them who have been sanctioned. Jobseekers can get a reduced rate (40 per cent of standard JSA or 20 per cent if a family member is seriously ill or pregnant) if they can show that they or a member of their family will suffer from no Jobseeker's Allowance (JSA). 'Vulnerable Groups' are eligible for this rate – they are carers, those with children, people who are pregnant or have pregnant partners, people who are disabled or chronically sick, and those with significant caring responsibilities. If someone has children, the child rates of JSA will continue to be paid. People can still claim Housing Benefit and Council Tax Benefit when sanctioned.

44 Inland Revenue, *Personal wealth*, 2002.

45 W. Paxton, *Wealth distribution – the evidence*, IFS, 2002.

46 J. Byrner and S. Despotidou, 'Effects of assets on life chances' (2001), quoted in J. Le Grand, *Motivation, agency and public policy,* Oxford University Press, 2003.

47 These perspectives are discussed in Le Grand, *Motivation, agency and public policy.*

48 See, for example, Claire Kober and Will Paxton (eds), *Asset-based welfare and poverty: Exploring the case for and against asset-based welfare policies,* End Child Poverty/IPPR, 2002.

49 D. Gordon and C. Pantazis, *Breadline Britain survey*, 1997.

50 M. Barnes, 'Reaching the socially excluded', in Kober and Paxton, *Asset-based welfare and poverty*, p. 14.

3 | Condemning a little less and understanding a little more

Nicholas Hillman, Policy Exchange

Introduction

The Joseph Rowntree Foundation's work on disadvantage over the next 20 years provides a timely, wide-ranging and useful assessment of the deep and consistent poverty that remains all too common in some areas and among some groups within the UK. As a review of current problems, it is depressing. But it is also challenging because the specific policy proposals that are put forward have great potential for reducing disadvantage.

Nonetheless, certain challenges, such as the needs of people who have been out of touch with the labour market for a long time and the impact of migration, are dealt with in too cursory a fashion. Moreover, while the problems associated with mass means-testing are identified, the assessment of current government policies on taxes and benefits is too uncritical.

This chapter begins with a discussion of poverty definitions and their relationship to benefit rates, particularly for adults who do not work. The following sections propose a number of ways to improve the employment prospects of disadvantaged people and to relieve financial poverty among children and pensioners. The fourth section considers the impact of migration, and current and future pressures on the housing market. The chapter ends with a short conclusion.

Poverty lines and benefit rates

The broad-brush picture of disadvantaged people and

communities painted by the Joseph Rowntree Foundation is of particular relevance to people on the right because it shows in stark relief the serious social problems that persisted – and in many instances worsened – as the economy grew after 1979. Above all, the enormous growth in inequality sits against the remarkable things that were achieved during the 1980s.

Some people still argue that inequality does not matter very much. A recent newspaper article claimed, 'It is unfortunate but inevitable that a small underclass of lazy, maladjusted or otherwise unfortunate individuals will continue to live desperate lives in spite of our opportunity economy and the safety net of the welfare state.'[1] In an interview during the 2001 general election, Tony Blair denied that the gap between rich and poor is important,[2] and, indeed, the main indicator of income inequality – the Gini coefficient – has risen since 1997.[3]

But it does matter. Ever greater inequality shatters the bonds that bind society together. Polly Toynbee has made the point by comparing recent performance to a caravan crossing a desert. As the procession has moved forward, the people at the back have gone far more slowly than those at the front: 'When the front and back are stretched so far apart, at what point can they no longer be said to be travelling together at all, breaking the community between them?'[4]

So the *Tackling disadvantage* project is right to begin with a discussion of relative poverty measures. And the favoured poverty line of 60 per cent of contemporary median income is at least as good as any other headline indicator for it is comparatively simple, used internationally and in line with the government's Public Service Agreement on child poverty.[5]

The information a single measure provides is of course limited, but the alternative of relying solely on lots of separate indicators is confusing and makes it difficult to hold the government to account. Ministers often dodge simple questions on poverty levels by referring to the range of indicators in the annual *Opportunity for all* report.[6] These other measurements are important, but a headline poverty line should help, rather than hinder, our understanding of other indicators.

Some Conservatives, in particular, fall into the trap of describing those living below the poverty line as feckless and unworthy of more support. But many of the 9.7 million people living in households on less than 60 per cent of median income[7] are non-working parents of young children, people with disabilities and pensioners. This explains why a recent research project into the dynamics of poverty concluded that 'an anti-poverty policy based around labour market measures is not sufficient to help many members of society for whom it is widely agreed that availability for paid work is not expected.'[8]

If poverty is relative, and if many people are not in a position to work, it follows that some benefits must sometimes be uprated by more than price inflation. People are familiar with the idea of fiscal drag, where increases in personal tax allowances do not keep up with earnings growth and more people end up in higher tax brackets. But, at the other end of the income distribution, there is poverty drag. If some major benefits only ever go up with prices, more people than otherwise will be in relative poverty.[9]

If individual benefits for people who are out of work cannot be forever linked to prices, other tricky issues emerge, such as the relationship between wages, in-work tax credits and out-of-work benefits. But as the Rowntree report, *Tackling UK poverty and disadvantage in the twenty-first century,* says, 'It is a nettle that, in time, will have to be grasped.'[10] And it will eventually need to be grasped by those on the right, as well as by supporters of the government.

Education and work

As we have seen, there are limits to any programme that seeks to relieve poverty via work, but the labour market is still the most powerful tool in reducing disadvantage. Research into the first nine waves of the British Household Panel Survey concluded, 'Changes in a household's labour earnings accounted for the largest share of exits from poverty.'[11]

The debate in this area has moved on considerably from the days when, as a young MP, Gordon Brown criticised conditionality in benefits for the unemployed as 'an insult to the workless',[12] but one particular myth remains prevalent. It is common to believe that the number of people who are out of work is small and has fallen considerably in recent years. That is not accurate. Unemployment has roughly halved over the last ten years to around 1.5 million people, but there are five times as many economically inactive people of working age than there are unemployed people and the latter group has grown modestly but consistently over the past decade.[13] In recent years, the government has moved away from the simplistic claimant count unemployment figures in favour of the higher International Labour Organisation survey measure, but we now need a further shift towards the figures on economic inactivity if we are to acknowledge properly one of the main causes of poverty.

As suggested in the previous section, many of the 8 million or so economically inactive people of working age are not in a position to work: some are in full-time education; others are parents of young children; and some are severely disabled. Nonetheless, over 2 million of them say they would like to work[14] and it is surprising that recent economic success has not brought more of them into the workforce. A successful poverty reduction strategy would be responsive to their needs, as well as to the needs of Jobseeker's Allowance claimants.

The most innovative and interesting of the New Deal programmes is the New Deal for Disabled People. Under this voluntary programme, jobseekers are assigned Job Brokers, who are often from the private or voluntary sectors and have considerable freedom in placing their clients into work. Unfortunately, the scheme has not been properly resourced in comparison with the other New Deals. According to the Select Committee on Work and Pensions:

> *less than £50 million have been spent on the New Deal for Disabled People since 1997, compared to £139 million for lone parents, nearly £500 million for those over 25 and over £1.3 billion for those under 25. Yet, there are now more people on incapacity-related benefits than there are lone parents or unemployed people claiming benefits ... That pattern of resources would be unlikely to have arisen if spending had developed in relation to the numbers involved – in other words, if local offices had been able to decide who to help from amongst their local population, according to need.*[15]

The Employment Zones initiative, which is focused on particularly impoverished areas, is another scheme which uses the experiences and ideas of people outside central government in a more effective way than the main New Deal programmes.[16] There is only a limited amount of information available on the scheme's record so far but,[17] as Nicholas Timmins has noted, 'it is already clear that the more freedom the private sector has had to innovate, the better the results have been.'[18]

Over the next few years, the flexible support that is offered through the New Deal for Disabled People and the Employment Zones should be offered to greater numbers of seriously disadvantaged people. This help could be targeted by ensuring that rewards for job placement depend both on the level of deprivation in an area and on the specific obstacles to work faced by individual jobseekers. In addition, there is scope for learning from initiatives abroad in areas such as offering jobseekers a choice of providers.[19] It is likely that this approach would prove more effective and cost efficient than the majority of existing New Deal programmes.

Another way to improve the work incentives of economically inactive people is to reduce the differences between their treatment and that of unemployed people.

For example, men aged 60 to 64 are currently entitled to the guarantee element of the Pension Credit, which is worth much more and has fewer strings attached than Jobseeker's Allowance. Around 20 per cent of all Guarantee Credit expenditure goes to men in this age group, even though they make up only about 10 per cent of the total caseload and are not officially classified as pensioners.[20] The rewards from work would be clearer for people in this group if their out-of-work benefit entitlement was more comparable with the entitlement of everyone else below state pension age. This could have a knock-on effect on female Guarantee Credit claimants aged 60 to 64, who do count as pensioners, but they make up a small proportion of the caseload and existing cases could be offered transitional protection.[21] The potentially large savings could then be used either to fund the welfare to work improvements or to provide more generous support for those aged 65 and over.

The differences between the benefits available to unemployed people and economically inactive people with disabilities could be reduced in a similar manner. One idea worth considering, which has been proposed by UnumProvident, is to introduce a new benefit called Jobseeker's Allowance Plus for people who are currently on Incapacity Benefit but who are capable of some work.[22]

A third way to facilitate the move into work would be to extend and improve the Social Fund. There is a consensus of opinion that the scheme is not working properly. For example, the National Association of Citizens Advice Bureaux (NACAB) has described the current situation as 'intolerable' and has argued that 'The way in which the Discretionary Social Fund operates at present means that it is not playing its part in combating poverty and social exclusion.'[23]

People on low incomes who have moved into work are not currently entitled to Social Fund Budgeting Loans or Community Care Grants. Yet there is good evidence to show that the first month in work is particularly difficult financially because of the gap between the last benefit payment and the first receipt of wages and because of new work-related expenses.[24] People in this position need better access to low cost credit.[25]

Any overhaul of Social Fund loans should at least extend the support available to families where one parent moves into a low-paid job. This could be done by making all households in receipt of the maximum Child Tax Credit eligible for Budgeting Loans and Community Care Grants, as proposed by NACAB.[26] The costs of such a change would be limited because any additional loans would still have to be paid back. At the same time, the government should also consider delivering Social Fund loans in a new, less humiliating way that is more comparable to private financial services.

Ideas of this sort are not new. For example, the Treasury published a report in 1999 that called for similar improvements to the Social Fund to be in place by the end of 2003.[27] At the time, ministers announced 'immediate action',[28] but little has happened since and the changes are now long overdue – despite pressure from the Commons Work and Pensions Committee.[29]

Children and pensioners

The Government's two most substantial changes to social security have been the introduction of the Child Tax Credit and the Pension Credit. The former has extended means testing to around nine out of ten families with dependent children, and the latter has reversed at a stroke the progress that was achieved in reducing the proportion of pensioners on means tests over the previous 20 years.[30]

Tackling disadvantage wisely identifies some of the significant problems associated with mass means-testing, including unwelcome behavioural effects, issues about stigma and low take-up.[31] Yet it is still too optimistic about the recent reforms and their capacity to relieve financial poverty.[32]

For example, too much credence is given to the Government's claims to have simplified the assessment of income. In reality, the actual means tests are at least as onerous as before. Claimants for the Child Tax Credit and the Working Tax Credit have to claim on the basis of income from a previous tax year and then make a new claim if their circumstances have changed in certain ways – the Government's own figures suggest that around 2 million out of the 6 million households claiming the tax credits will fall into this trap.[33] These people's claims are then based on forecast, rather than actual, income and many of them will still have to settle up at the end of the year. Other work for the Joseph Rowntree Foundation shows that end-of-year reconciliation causes all sorts of problems for families in Australia and it is likely to cause nightmares here as well.[34]

Similarly, for many older people the Pension Credit will not actually be fixed for five years as the Government claims. It is estimated that each year 11 per cent of the Pension Credit caseload will be admitted to hospital and 10 per cent will be admitted to a care home, thereby affecting their entitlement.[35] Others will have changes to their level of savings and this will also affect the amount of money they can receive because the Government has chosen not to abandon the old capital rules, as they originally promised, but simply to modify them instead.[36]

A means-tested safety net will be needed for a very long time to come, but the problems raised by the new credits suggest that the inherent difficulties of income related benefits are not easily ironed out. They also provide a real obstacle to the idea put forward by Donald Hirsch and David Darton of introducing a new income-related retirement pension with a maximum and minimum rate.[37]

The irony about the government's reforms is that the two groups most affected by the enormous extension of means testing – children and pensioners – were already targeted by successful, popular and universal benefits. Despite the declining importance of these benefits in recent years, it is likely that they continue to offer a better long-term model than excessively complicated means tests that cover huge swathes of people.

Around half of the 5.75 million families entitled to the Child Tax Credit are only entitled to the £545 family element. To claim their £10 a week, they have to go through the same horrendously complicated and costly assessment procedure as poorer families do to claim their higher payments. There is a strong argument that a similar distributional impact could be achieved in simpler ways.

For example, through a new child tax allowance or, if it was deemed important that the money should go to the caring parent and that independent taxation should be reinforced, through a higher Child Benefit payment for the first child, with accompanying changes to the residual Child Tax Credit. If necessary, the 10 per cent of families with children in receipt of the highest incomes could still be frozen out in some way, for example by gradual withdrawal of the new child tax allowance.

Of course, structural changes have limited value if they seek merely to replicate the existing income distribution. But a simpler system in which fewer households are means tested can be targeted much more effectively. For example, 62 per cent of children (1.7 million) living below the poverty line are in households headed by a couple.[38] Yet, in contrast with traditional means-tested benefits (and the government's own low income statistics), the new tax credits do not recognise the extra costs of a second adult being present.[39] If second adults were taken into account in some way when calculating entitlement, this would help relieve child poverty, discourage the common fraud of partners pretending not to be a couple[40] and bolster relationships. But recognising a second adult within all households eligible for the existing Child Tax Credit is prohibitively expensive. If, however, the measure was restricted to low-income families, as outlined above, it would be far cheaper and easier to do.[41]

In addition, there is a need for some detailed social research into the effect of tax credits on gross pay. People on both the left and the right have criticised in-work benefits of the type favoured by Gordon Brown for encouraging employers to pay less than market wages. In the original parliamentary debate on the bill that introduced the world's first modern in-work benefit, the Family Income Supplement of 1971 to 1988, the Labour amendment raised this fear, as did Enoch Powell, who claimed that 'a man should receive as near as may be the full value of his work in cash.'[42] More recently, Polly Toynbee criticised the Working Families Tax Credit that was in place between 1999 and 2003 in similar terms: 'Without WFTC employers would have to put up wages until they made it worth people's while to go back to work.'[43] Yet little has been done to investigate the existence or size of such effects, despite the massive expansion of in-work benefits, the move towards channelling the money through people's pay packets and the introduction of the National Minimum Wage. Research comparing areas covered by the Earnings Top-up, a pilot in-work benefit for people without children which existed from 1996 to 1999, to areas that were not covered, found a small impact on wages, but the conclusions were tentative and are of uncertain relevance to the current situation.[44]

Pensioners would also benefit from a dose of simplification. Among the benefits they currently receive from the state are the Graduated Retirement Pension, the State Earnings Related Pension, the State Second Pension, the basic state pension, the Minimum Income Guarantee and a number of special payments. In addition, there are disability benefits, benefits in kind and other means-tested payments. This structure is so complicated that it is very difficult for pensioners to claim what is rightfully theirs and for working age people to make sensible decisions about saving.

Instead of searching for entirely new solutions, we should seek in this area to build on the existing consensus in favour of more generous state provision, less means testing and greater incentives to save. The Pensions Policy Institute have highlighted the similarities between the various reform models that have already been put forward by organisations such as the Association of British Insurers,

Age Concern and the Institute for Public Policy Research: 'That the proposed reforms seek to make the UK state pension system more universal and more generous reflects that all want to reverse the likely future trend if there was no intervention.'[45] The problem is that we still lack precise details about the full costs, the distributional impact and the practical details of moving from the current system, which is inexorably extending means testing, to a more universal one that does more to reward saving.

It is time to consider reforms that have the potential to meet both the desires of those who want to see a radical reduction in the amount of means testing of pensioners' incomes and the concerns of politicians who fear the sort of sudden sharp increase in benefit expenditure that many of the proposals envisage. One way to do this might be to raise the basic state pension to the level of the Minimum Income Guarantee for a restricted group of pensioners and then to gradually extend the new policy downwards as resources allow. It would have cost £1.7 billion to apply this policy to pensioners aged over 80 in 2003/04, which is similar to the cost of the Winter Fuel Payments.[46] This policy would have a big impact on the number of people entitled to means-tested benefits, for older pensioners tend to be poorer than others. Moreover, because all three main political parties have argued in the recent past that older pensioners should receive additional support, it has a comparatively good chance of being implemented.

Immigration and housing

The JRF working paper, *Tackling disadvantage*, identifies 'relatively high numbers of immigrants' as an important factor related to poverty,[47] but does not consider the issue in much detail. The official prediction for future annual net inward migration into the United Kingdom is regularly altered and, although it has recently been revised downwards from 135,000 people to 100,000 people a year,[48] the figure remains substantial. The gross number of immigrants will, of course, be significantly higher than this and, if the figure is the predicted 180,000 a year, then over the next 20 years there will be around 3.6 million immigrants in total.

The sort of impact that migration on this scale can have is reflected in recent labour market statistics, which show that the number of people who are economically active and the number of people who are economically inactive have been rising together. Between 1993 and 2003, the total working age population grew by 1.7 million.[49]

The Home Office has recently made an assessment of the net annual fiscal impact of first-generation legal immigrants. Their conclusions are optimistic: 'it is estimated that migrants in the UK contributed £31.2 billion in taxes, and increased public expenditure by £28.8 billion through their receipt of public goods and services, resulting in an estimated net fiscal contribution of around £2.5 billion.'[50]

But the same report also notes that migrants to the UK are heterogeneous, and treating all of them together conceals some very big differences. Given the nature of the British labour market, skilled people are likely to find it relatively easy to secure employment, and indeed 'migrants are prevalent at the high end of the earnings distribution.'[51] Many other migrants, however, are concentrated at the other end of the spectrum. For example, a comparatively high proportion of people coming to the UK have no qualifications and there is a strong correlation between educational achievement and economic performance.[52] Many of these people have been welcomed to the country for humanitarian reasons and have as much right as everyone else to be here, but we should not pretend that they have little bearing on poverty rates.

It has been suggested that the greatest impact of unskilled migrants is on the previously resident, unskilled population. For example, Richard Layard, Co-Director of the Centre for Economic Performance, has noted:

> *For European employers and skilled workers, unskilled immigration brings real advantages. It provides labour for their restaurants, building sites and car parks and helps to keep these services cheap by keeping down the wages of those who work there. But for unskilled Europeans it is a mixed blessing. It depresses their wages and may affect their job opportunities ... We need to allow for the different interests at stake. And for unskilled people these interests run beyond wages and jobs – into housing, schooling and the rest.*[53]

Similarly, the House of Lords Select Committee on the European Union has argued that illegal immigration 'can make it more difficult for the less skilled sections of the resident population to find jobs ... [and] tends to lower wage levels and employment standards'.[54]

Past research on migration has thrown up a number of contradictory conclusions[55] and considerably more work is needed before detailed predictions can be made on the impact of future immigration. Nonetheless, we need to recognise that any holistic assessment of future poverty rates within the UK must look closely at migration trends and that poverty rates in developing countries are also likely to be affected by the mass movement of people across national boundaries. At the very least, the Government should do more to track down the huge number of people who have been refused asylum but who have not left the country.

In conjunction with other expected demographic trends, such as a continuing growth in single person households, future immigration on the scale predicted by the Government is likely to have a particular impact on the demand for housing. There is already substantial pent-up pressure for new housing. This is reflected in the high prices in many regions, in the tens of thousands of homeless households in temporary accommodation[56] and in the substandard quality of many people's homes. In short, it is clear that the gap between the number of dwellings of acceptable quality that are needed and those that are available is large and growing.

Perhaps the biggest obstacle to solving this problem is nimbyism, or the 'not in my backyard' syndrome. This is particularly difficult to tackle because settled communities are prone to campaign strongly against developments that could change the nature of their area. But there is no counterweight pressure from the people who would move into the area afterwards. Some sites are obviously not appropriate for new housing, but the current strength of nimbyism reinforces housing inequality by keeping prices high, reducing mobility and reinforcing the social division between inner cities and elsewhere. As Chris Holmes, the former director of Shelter, has pointed out, 'it is important to distinguish between what are legitimate concerns over damage to the environment or inappropriate housing proposals, and what is straightforward selfish opposition to encroachment by newcomers into desirable communities.'[57]

Politicians, at both national and local level, need to tackle this issue by making a positive case for the wider benefits of more socially diverse communities, by avoiding the temptation to make party political capital out of opposing sensible new developments and by explaining more clearly why it is necessary to build on some of the low-quality land that is within greenfield areas.

Tackling nimbyism holds the key to relieving some of the demand for housing, but it will be of limited use in rejuvenating deprived inner city areas. The pressures on these areas are so immense that no single initiative is going to solve them, but one surprising failure of the urban housing market is the relative lack of accommodation that is targeted specifically at the large and growing number of young graduates who move into urban areas each year to start their careers. In general, these people do not have the capital or the desire to purchase their own property.

The Joseph Rowntree Foundation's CASPAR (City-centre Apartments for Single People at Affordable Rents) developments in Birmingham and Leeds[58] suggest that the potential rewards for private companies and others of providing modern and secure accommodation that is halfway between a hall of residence and a city apartment and which is designed specifically for young graduates could be very substantial. This is likely to be particularly true where the accommodation is situated in cheaper areas. Housing of this type could play an important role in altering the social mix and age profile of inner city communities, in attracting public sector workers to deprived areas and in rejuvenating local economies. As well as having relatively high incomes, the graduates would be unlikely to make much call on local public services, such as schools and hospitals, and many of them might choose to remain in the area once they are in a position to purchase their own property.

Conclusion

The challenges involved in tackling unacceptable levels of inequality are likely to be immense over the next 20 years. But, as *Tackling disadvantage* argues, if we do not begin to map out a strategy now, high poverty rates will go on limiting the potential of millions of people on low incomes, as well as harming the interests of the wider community.

Poverty is about more than income, but many of the problems faced by people who are socially excluded will not be solved unless they have more money. If poverty is also deemed to be relative, rather than absolute, then it has to be accepted that out-of-work benefits for non-working adults must sometimes be raised by more than price inflation.

But changing the way in which benefits are increased can only have a limited impact on the incidence and depth of poverty. We also need to recognise that, for many people, the best way to tackle poverty is to improve incentives to work. Now that unemployment is at manageable levels, we should focus new initiatives on the millions of people who do not work, but who also do not appear in the unemployment figures. This means building on the most successful of the existing welfare to work schemes and reducing some of the differences between the benefit conditions for unemployed people, and the rules for others who are not in employment, but who could do some work. It also means making it easier for people to jump the financial hurdles associated with moving into work after a long period on benefit by, for example, improving access to the Social Fund.

The structure of government support for children and pensioners on low incomes has been changed significantly in the last few years. In general, it has become more generous, but it has also become much more reliant on means testing, and considerably more complicated. As a result, in poverty reduction terms, the Government has seen little return for its extra spending. Given the difficulties associated with the introduction of the new tax credits and the Pension Credit and the need for the new system to bed down, there is a case for not overhauling benefits in a radical way for at least a few years, but there is also an urgent need to reduce means testing. This could mean replacing the Child Tax Credit at the top end as a prelude to recognising the needs of children in two-parent families on low incomes and simplifying the benefit entitlement of pensioners through improvements to the basic state pension.

The challenges posed by mass migration are unlikely to reduce in coming years and, although the precise effects are unclear, this could have a particular impact on unskilled British people, on the quality of life for the immigrants themselves and even on poverty rates in some developing countries. There is no simple answer to these issues, but a successful poverty reduction strategy for the next 20 years needs to recognise them more explicitly than has always been the case in the past. For example, the increase in population resulting from migration into Britain, along with the continuing growth in single person households and the existing backlog of housing need, calls for a much braver approach to housing policy. In particular, there is a need to promote public debate on developing certain greenfield sites and to weaken the impact of nimbyism. Within cities, the housing needs of young professionals could be partly met through new developments on otherwise undesirable brownfield sites and this could help to increase the social and age mix of deprived areas, while stimulating the local economy without placing much additional pressure on local public services.

There is every reason to hope that new proposals of this type, in conjunction with the ideas in *Tackling disadvantage*, would have a big impact on future poverty rates, but it is equally important to remember that they are unlikely to be enough on their own. Other factors – for example, big increases in taxation on lower income households[59] – could push in the opposite direction. Above all, any long-term poverty reduction strategy needs to be flexible enough to respond to new opposing pressures and unexpected events.

Notes

Nicholas Hillman thanks David Willetts MP, Shadow Secretary of State for Work and Pensions, Nicholas Boles, Director of Policy Exchange, Mike Brewer, Senior Research Economist at the Institute for Fiscal Studies and Joanne Segars OBE, Head of Pensions and Savings at the Association of British Insurers, for their comments on a draft of this chapter.

1   Ross Clark, 'The Tories turn into the party of silly beggars', *The Times*, 20 May 2003.

2   Tony Blair interview on *Newsnight*, 4 June 2001, available at http://news.bbc.co.uk/1/hi/events/newsnight/1372220.stm.

3   See www.statistics.gov.uk/CCI/nugget.asp?ID=332&Pos=&ColRank =2&Rank=672; Andrew Shephard, *Inequality under the Labour government*, Institute for Fiscal Studies, March 2003.

4   Polly Toynbee, *Hard work: Life in low-pay Britain*, Bloomsbury, 2003, pp. 3–4.

5   HM Treasury, *Technical note for HM Treasury's Public Service Agreement (PSA) 2003–2006*, November 2002, p. 24.

6   See, for example, the reply from Malcolm Wicks MP to David Laws MP, *Hansard*, 20 July 2001, col. 694W.

7   Department for Work and Pensions (DWP), *Households below average income: An analysis of the income distribution from 1994/95 to 2001/02*, March 2003, pp. 37, 65, 115.

8   Stephen P. Jenkins and John A. Rigg, *The dynamics of poverty in Britain*, DWP, Research Report no.157, December 2001, p. 107.

9   There is some evidence to suggest that the main benefits not dependent on the presence of children fell against the Retail Prices Index between 1996/97 and 2000/01. See Holly Sutherland, Tom Sefton and David Piachaud, *Poverty in Britain: The impact of government policy since 1997*, JRF, October 2003, table 9.

10 David Utting, 'Breaking the links between family poverty and social exclusion', in David Darton and Jason Strelitz (eds), *Tackling UK poverty and disadvantage in the twenty-first century: An exploration of the issues*, JRF, February 2003, p.80.

11 Stephen P. Jenkins and John A. Rigg, *The dynamics of poverty in Britain*, DWP, Research Report No.157, December 2001, p.107.

12 Quoted in Paul Routledge, *Gordon Brown: The biography*, Pocket Books, 1998, p. 120.

13 Labour Force Survey (www.statistics.gov.uk/downloads/theme_ labour/ LMS_FR_HS/Table13.xls).

14 Labour Force Survey (www.statistics.gov.uk/downloads/theme_labour/ LMS_FR_HS/Table14.xls).

15 Work and Pensions Committee, *Employment for all: Interim report*, April 2003, para.16. More recent figures on the cost of the various New Deal programmes, including forecast expenditure for future years, are available in DWP, *Departmental report 2003*, May 2003, table 7.

16 Stephen Martin, 'Free the PA!', in The Work Foundation, *Full employment and the New Deal*, pp. 17–22.

17 See, however, Andy Hirst et al., *Employment zones: A study of local delivery agents and case studies*, DWP, Working Age Evaluation Report no.124, July 2002.

18 Nicholas Timmins, 'Why public services harbour private worries', *Financial Times*, 17 June 2002.

19 Dan Finn, *Privatising employment assistance: Lessons from the Australian Job Network*, paper presented to the Inclusion and Work Foundation Seminar, 11 July 2002.

20 Author's own calculations based on the Department for Work and Pensions/Office of National Statistics, *Income Support quarterly statistical enquiry: May 2003*, September 2003, tables 2.1 and 2.6.

21 DWP/ONS, *Income Support quarterly statistical enquiry: May 2003*, September 2003, table 2.1.

22 Unum Ltd, *Diversity in employment – the strategic direction of work, benefits and employment policy*, December 2001.

23 NACAB, *Unfair and underfunded: CAB evidence on what's wrong with the Social Fund*, October 2002, p. 1.

24 Tim Harries and Kandy Woodfield, *Easing the transition to work*, DWP, Research Report no. 175, October 2002.

25 Christopher Farrell and William O'Connor, *Low-income families and household spending*, DWP, Research Report no.192, July 2003, p. 75.

26 NACAB, *Unfair and underfunded*, pp. 14–16.

27 Policy Action Team 14, *Access to financial services*, HM Treasury, November 1999, pp. 56–7.

28 Ibid., Foreword.

29 Work and Pensions Committee, *The Social Fund,* April 2001, para. 123.

30 ONS/The Pensions Group, *The pensioners' incomes series*, June 2003, figure 12 and table A9.

31 Donald Hirsch and David Darton, 'Combining opportunity and

support', in Darton and Strelitz, *Tackling UK poverty*, pp. 109–111.

32 Ibid., p. 111.

33 H.M. Treasury, *The Child and Working Tax Credits*, April 2002, pp. 28–9.

34 'Tax credits and how to respond to income changes', JRF *Findings* ref. 543, May 2003.

35 *Hansard*, 17 July 2003, col. 557W.

36 Claimants are now assumed to receive £1 a week income for every £500 of savings over £6,000, rather than £1 for every £250.

37 Hirsch and Darton, 'Combining opportunity and support', p. 118.

38 Before housing costs, including the self employed; DWP, *Households below average income*, figure 4.4.

39 For further information on how one-parent and two-parent families are treated by the tax and benefit systems, see DWP/ONS, *Tax benefit model tables: April 2003*, July 2003.

40 John Bourn, *Comptroller and Auditor General's standard report on the accounts of the Inland Revenue 2002–3,* National Audit Office, November 2003, page 75.

41 The author is grateful to Leonard Beighton and Don Draper, consultants to CARE, whose research and ideas on the tax credit entitlement of different families have influenced this section.

42 *Hansard*, 10 November 1970, cols 230, 264–5.

43 Toynbee, *Hard work*, p. 235.

44 Alan Marsh, *Earnings top-up evaluation: synthesis report*, DWP, Research Report no. 135, January 2001, chapter 4.

45 Pensions Policy Institute, *A guide to state pension reform*, July 2003, p. 48.

46 *Hansard*, 13 February 2003, col. 964W; www.dwp.gov.uk/asd/asd4/Table1.xls.

47 'Introduction: the unsolved problem within the UK's economic success', in Darton and Strelitz, *Tackling UK poverty*, pp. 14 and 44.

48 See www.gad.gov.uk/Population/2001/methodology/migrass.htm; Chris Shaw, 'Interim 2001-based national population projections for the United Kingdom and constituent countries', *Population Trends*, 111, Spring 2003, p. 10.

49 Labour Force Survey (www.statistics.gov.uk/downloads/theme_labour/LMS_FR_HS/Table01.xls).

50 Ceri Gott and Karl Johnston, *The migrant population in the UK: Fiscal effects*, Home Office, Research, Development and Statistics Directorate, Occasional Paper no. 77, February 2002, p. 11.

51 Ibid., p. 9.

52 Ibid., p. 10 and figure 8.

53 Richard Layard, 'Conflict between Europe and migrant labour', *Financial Times*, 20 May 2002.

54 European Union Committee, *A common policy on illegal immigration*, November 2002, para. 32.

55 See, for example, the discussion about the impact of immigration on wage rates and unemployment in Anthony Browne, 'Cost of the migration revolution', *The Times*, 1 March 2003.

56 Statistics on the number of homeless households in temporary accommodation are available at www.odpm.gov.uk/stellent/ groups/odpm_control/documents/contentservertemplate/odpm_in dex.hcst?n=855&l=1.

57 Chris Holmes, *Housing, equality and choice*, Institute of Public Policy Research, August 2003, p. 21.

58 For further information, see www.jrf.org.uk/housingandcare/ caspar/.

59 The Government's poverty statistics do not take indirect taxes into account, despite their generally regressive nature. For this reason, poverty rates have probably fallen by slightly less than government figures suggest since 1997. See Sutherland, Sefton and Piachaud, *Poverty in Britain*, chapter 5.

4 | Beyond the bounds

Resources for tackling disadvantage

*Jim McCormick, Fiona Spencer and Corinna Gamble,
Scottish Council Foundation*

Introduction

Despite the 'quietly' redistributive effects of Labour budgets since 1997, and the high priority that the Scottish Executive has attached to social justice, trends in key areas continue to reflect wide inequalities in Scotland in income and wealth. The overall burden of poverty is estimated to have fallen, but not as far as hoped.[1] A similar pattern is seen in terms of health outcomes: Scotland has the slowest rate of improvement in life expectancy in western Europe, after Portugal, and among the widest inequalities in health within the UK.

Scotland continues to experience the pressures felt elsewhere in the UK: a decline in the demand for lower skilled labour, the increasing importance of core skills in all kinds of jobs, the growth in numbers of households (especially single adult households) and increased longevity. In addition, it faces a more challenging demographic position because it has one of the lowest birth rates in western Europe and a low level of immigration. These factors combine with changing patterns of working and living. Many more women over the age of 50 are in employment, for example, challenging traditional assumptions about who can do the unpaid work of caring. The willingness of the Scottish Executive to make major commitments, such as the provision of personal care for the elderly without charge, sends a clear signal about the kind of society to which we aspire.

However, there is a risk of failing to address associated issues, such as pressures on other public services, so that instead of reducing disadvantage we simply change its pattern. One risk in particular is the re-emergence of poverty in old age as incomes and assets fail to stretch far enough across longer lives.

From the work carried out by the Scottish Council Foundation (SCF) in 2000–3, we can identify some ways in which the causes and consequences of poverty could be tackled in the long term, by focusing on what people need to enjoy prosperous lives. In our view, a 20-year strategy to tackle disadvantage should address market failure as well as failures in public services. This is an important element in ensuring that more people experience more of the benefits and fewer of the risks of living in an affluent society, as in certain European neighbours or G8 members like Finland, the Netherlands, France, Germany and Canada. Some of the defining features of a prosperous society – choice, autonomy, and effective opportunities to earn, learn and save – fail to reach disadvantaged households and communities in a consistent way. Smarter action is needed not only to secure sources of income and a wider spread of financial assets, but also to achieve high quality services such as nursery education, with the close involvement of families, and money advice services aiming to address, as well as limit, the seriousness of financial problems.

The common assumption in Scotland that reducing poverty is beyond the powers of local government and the Scottish Executive, and of little interest to the private sector, deserves to be challenged. An example is the final evaluation of *New Life for Urban Scotland* (published by the Scottish Executive in 1999), a 10-year regeneration strategy in four low-income housing estates, ending in 1998, which argued that there are clear limits to how far area regeneration can tackle poverty:

> *A key issue for regeneration is the high levels*
> *and concentration of poverty on these estates. In*
> *a superficial sense, it is true to say that the way*
> *to alleviate poverty is to raise incomes. But that*
> *should not be an objective of regeneration*
> *programmes ... The appropriate objective for*
> *alleviating poverty is the equalising of access to*
> *life chances, such as adequate support,*
> *employment opportunities, good health, sound*
> *education, inclusion in society and good housing*
> *... It is not open to area-based schemes to opt for*
> *a direct financial approach ... The nearest might*
> *be those measures that local bodies can take to*
> *improve take-up of benefits and services by*
> *outreach to excluded groups and individuals.*

This reflects, at best, a partial recognition of what can be achieved. There are few signs that Social Inclusion Partnerships (SIPs) have been able to take a more ambitious approach. Government and its partner agencies can go further than delivering more accurate advice on benefit take-up. By seeking to improve local conditions for private services to function, government agencies can play a vital gatekeeping role, improving access to affordable services and helping to develop sustainable opportunities for private services where markets are currently weak.

Different tiers of government have various policy instruments at their disposal to tackle disadvantage. Both Westminster and Holyrood can combine more effectively to achieve better outcomes. The UK government can reduce poverty through earnings (welfare to work, minimum wage), in-work benefits, tax credits and other improvements in welfare benefits, particularly for families with children and the retired poor, while the Scottish Executive could also address poverty by helping to deliver reductions across a series of high costs facing low-income households for basic goods and services.

In this response to the JRF report, *Tackling disadvantage,* we outline in brief what it currently means for people to lack a fair share of the prosperity enjoyed by many. We then offer some proposals for addressing this by tackling market failure and weakening the root causes of deep and enduring forms of poverty. These are reflected in the cumulative effects that are particularly characteristic of Scotland, where disadvantage in one sphere, such as income poverty or health, tends to spill over into housing, education or lifetime earnings.[2] We identify ways in which disadvantage could be tackled through measures to promote inclusion in mainstream financial services, as an example of how markets could function more effectively in low-income communities. We then consider different types of action across people's lives, recognising that although prevention of poverty from an early age is better than cure, cure in later life is better than neglect.

Trends in disadvantage

Our ability to 'map' the changing dimensions of poverty and analyse root causes has improved significantly in recent years. We believe that the dynamic nature of disadvantage means we should focus increasingly on net changes over time: as some people move out of poverty, others move in, and others still remain at risk. The fundamental challenge is, therefore, to shift the net trend downwards in a sustainable manner.

The following indicators summarise recent trends in disadvantage in Scotland:

- A higher proportion of children than adults are in poor households. Around 300,000 children living in Scotland (1 in 3) are estimated to be growing up in low-income households, and despite a reduction in recent years, around 200,000 are living in workless households.[3] The risk is higher among large families, for whom the benefits trap poses a serious problem. A recent study by the Centre for Research in Social Policy at Loughborough University shows that the poorest children are more likely to be found in families where adults move on and off benefits, in and out of work, or where there are changing family circumstances, not in households permanently on benefits.[4]

- A recent analysis for the UK as a whole concludes that relative poverty[5] fell by about 1 million across the 4-year period to 2000–1, with the numbers of poor children reduced by half a million. It forecasts that the numbers of poor children will be reduced by around 1 million in total by April 2004. In Scotland, the New Policy Institute's analysis suggests that little change in relative poverty levels occurred between the mid 1990s and 2000–1, although a slight upward trend could be discerned in the last four years. We can expect to see a modest decline in poverty in Scotland in the next round of data, as a result of higher employment rates and increased levels of some benefits. This is progress, but it is slow and brings the level of poverty back to a similar level to that recorded at the start of the 1990s. Moreover, it still leaves Scotland and the rest of Britain doing worse than all other EU countries except Greece,[6] and significantly worse than 20 years ago.

- A marked reduction in claims for means-tested benefits (mainly Income Support covering children, lone parents, disabled people and jobseekers) was recorded in the period 1997–2001. According to one analysis of the changing geography of poverty,[7] the reduction was greater in better-off areas, with the smallest improvement in poverty levels by this measure taking place in Scotland, as well as the North East and North of England, and South Wales. The proportion of working-age benefit claims has been falling in Scotland at about half the rate for Britain as a whole.

- At the same time, the *depth* of poverty (households on less than 50 per cent of the median income) grew slowly in the 4-year period to 2000–1.[8] While the number of people in poverty may now be falling, the relative severity of the problem for those worst affected may be the same.[9]

- It matters when poverty is experienced and for how long. US panel data stretching back over 30 years reveals that preschool poverty has the biggest negative impact on educational outcomes years later. According to British Household Panel Study (BHPS) data, almost half of children aged under 5 had some experience of poverty over a 6-year period in the 1990s, while 1 in 7 experienced chronic poverty (defined as remaining in poverty for all six years).[10] This clearly implies the need to cut the *duration* of poverty, especially in families with young children, as well as the 'headline' rate of poverty.

- The cumulative effect of Labour budgets since 1997 has been clearly redistributive, with the greatest tax/benefit gains targeted on the poorest 20 per cent of households. Nevertheless, income inequality has continued to grow, although at a slower rate than in the period 1979–92,[11] and remained at a slightly lower level in Scotland than in the rest of Britain by 2000–1.[12] The average incomes of the poorest 20 per cent grew at half the rate of the richest 20 per cent in the period 1997–2000. The sobering fact for those committed to reducing inequality as well as tackling exclusion is that even the significant changes announced in successive Labour Budgets since 1997 have had less of an impact on the long-run trend in the distribution of incomes than changes in earnings, savings and assets. While the full effect of various reforms (such as Children's Tax Credit and Employment Tax Credit) has still to be felt, we should not overlook the distinction between the intended consequences and the actual results of policy. We have seen a growing *complexity* of policy interventions in order to target resources more precisely, for instance the new Pension Credit as well as reforms for people of working age. This is problematic for levels of awareness and take-up. It is not clear that the current balance between universal and targeted approaches is the most effective in terms of achieving the desired outcomes of governments in Scotland and the rest of the UK.

- Trends in inequality need to be tracked over time, measured for example by the chances of progressing during the life cycle from the lowest 20 per cent of the income distribution to the middle 20 per cent. We know from BHPS data that low-income groups experience a considerable amount of 'churning',[13] but most of the movement is short distance, confined to the lower rungs of the income ladder. In this sense, the UK is not as mobile as some other OECD countries, and in relative terms it is not a more egalitarian society for those who begin life poor than it was 30 years ago.

In addition to this brief summary, we identify key policy choices still to be resolved:

- *Targeting or universalism*: no clear consensus has yet emerged from Labour in UK or Scottish government. For example, changes for retired people in recent years have included means-tested improvements in income (Minimum Income Guarantee and Pension Credit); modest across-the-board increases in the Basic State Pension; universal Winter Fuel Allowance; and free personal care costs for older people living in Scotland.

- *Reducing inequality or tackling exclusion*: it is possible to reduce some of the worst examples of economic and social exclusion, while income and wealth inequalities continue to grow. Indeed that appears to be happening in Scotland. Some commentators on the centre-left of politics argue that focusing on the gap between high and low earners diverts attention away from the task of improving conditions for the poorest. On the other hand, some international evidence suggests that high levels of inequality in the long term are correlated with wider health inequalities, lower than average life expectancy, lower levels of social trust and higher rates of violent crime.[14] We believe the issue of British levels of inequality cannot be set aside – and that the Scottish Executive's focus on social justice and 'closing the opportunity gap' suggests an explicit concern with *distributional* issues, as well as absolute improvements in outcomes for excluded groups. There is a clear need for better evidence on how economic and social policy might reduce inequality while also extending prosperity.

Related to this last point, we have found through recent qualitative research[15] that adults in Scotland tend not to express a clear view about 'social justice' as an organising principle, or even see reducing poverty as a priority. Emphasis on the insurance element of welfare and other policies, and on the Rawlsian principle of justice (roughly, if none of us knew anything about the future, what conditions would we choose to put in place to take care of all contingencies?) may provide a firm basis for progressive action, while politicians seek to develop social justice as a meaningful public interest concept.

Beyond the bounds: Actions to tackle disadvantage

As well as considering specific consequences of poverty in other reports,[16] the Scottish Council Foundation has looked in depth at statistical evidence that describes the changing 'map' of poverty. There is now a pressing need to focus on possible actions to extend prosperity more broadly, and tackle disadvantage. We see this approach as wholly distinct from relying on 'trickle down' economics to distribute eventually some benefits of growing affluence to all parts of society. This means identifying and tackling risk factors across the three related dimensions of depth, duration and concentration of disadvantage.

We now consider some actions that could go further than existing steps to tackle disadvantage, and how they should be organised. These are based mainly on findings from the SCF's research programme in 2000–3 and some of the themes to be developed in our future work.

An increasingly common approach is to align policy around stages in people's lives, from early childhood to retirement, coupled with a focus on disadvantaged communities.[17] While this has the merit of clarity, and specific policies are more relevant to some stages in the life course than others, we believe there is a risk that this approach could limit our understanding of how our lives are changing. For example, 'working age' and 'retirement' are likely to be redefined by significant changes in demography, the economy and social policy. In this response, we have chosen to present a number of actions in terms of the resources or assets that we believe need to be deployed more effectively. These resources are of value across people's lives, and of particular importance at times of transition and risk of poverty. We describe these as 'symbolic' actions, to be pursued in addition to reforms by the Scottish Executive and UK government that are already under way or proposed. They will help to make the reforms responsive to the changing reality of life and work.

Markets

The first resource we consider comes from the market, which could offer services that are more relevant, accessible and affordable. What does the private sector have to do with reducing poverty in Scotland? Despite brave talk about the potential for 'corporate social responsibility' to engage business more directly in the social justice agenda of government, it is the other CSR – the Comprehensive Spending Review, led in Whitehall by the Treasury – that has a more powerful bearing on how poor people in disadvantaged communities fare.

Research evidence shows that the lowest income households are disproportionately affected by market as well as public service failures. Not only do these households have less money coming in, they face relatively higher costs in money going out. Through a combination of regulation, private sector engagement with the inclusion agenda and local anti-poverty action, wider access to cheaper and higher quality services can be stimulated. This approach is more likely to succeed when public agencies, including social housing authorities, act as gatekeepers between the private sector and low-income households, pooling their combined purchasing power to create lower cost and viable market opportunities than currently exist on a household-by-household basis. Such an approach has been applied, though unevenly, to promoting financial inclusion.

More people than ever have bank accounts, insurance products and savings accounts. Financial exclusion has deepened rather than widened: those who are outside the system are smaller in number than in the past, but the consequences are harsher and the prospects for inclusion without coordinated government action are slim. Financial exclusion is both a consequence and a further cause of poverty.

The proportion of households without bank accounts or insurance is higher in Scotland than in the rest of Britain, despite the presence of a large and influential financial services sector. Financial exclusion matters because it restricts choice and increases basic costs. Households without a bank account end up paying more for basics like gas and electricity, because they are charged for paying in cash. There is no discount for those unable to pay by direct debit or on the internet. There are also high charges for using the growing number of cheque-cashing agencies. The uninsured run the risk of being unable to replace stolen or damaged home contents. When households like these need a loan to cope with an emergency they may have to turn to high cost moneylenders, unless they are members of a credit union or are eligible to receive a loan from the Social Fund. Moreover, financial exclusion makes it harder to get a job and keep it, more difficult to reduce debt and impossible to build up emergency savings.

While the consequences are clear, the problem of financial exclusion has no single cause. Exclusion is usually the result of a number of factors rather than simply a refusal by banks and insurance companies to serve poor customers. The withdrawal of bank branches from poor urban neighbourhoods and remote and rural communities has restricted the availability of products. A UK study of insurance cover found that most low-income households are excluded because the cost of premiums or home security improvements is too high.[18] There is little need for providers to engage in US-style 'red-lining' of communities with high crime rates because these other obstacles push insurance beyond the reach of many low-income households. To quote one insurer: 'There is no such thing as an uninsurable risk in Britain – just an unpayable premium.'

But there are solutions, and these are more likely to succeed if they focus on designing more appropriate products for the needs of households with only a little extra cash to spare, as well as providing new methods of selling and paying for products. Responsibility for this is shared between government and business: progress can be made without legislation, with the closer involvement of Scotland's banks and insurers.

Success in reducing financial exclusion is based on a simple analysis. Scotland's poorest communities tend to represent sizeable but poorly developed markets, which banks and insurers have been reluctant to serve on terms which low-income households can afford. One task is to develop markets using social housing landlords as intermediaries standing between tenants and the private sector. If social housing landlords are prepared to use their brokerage powers to manage the risks and negotiate pooled service packages for communities on more attractive terms than would be available to individual households, the worst features of financial exclusion can be reduced.

There are already practical examples. A large number of local authorities and a smaller but growing proportion of housing associations offer 'insure with rent' policies, allowing tenants to take out comprehensive home insurance for as little as £1.20 a week. Because premiums can be paid in regular cash instalments along with the rent, there is no need to have a bank account. Housing providers earn commission from insurers, which might be used to improve home security. Significantly, the most effective schemes involve mainstream insurers tailoring their products to fit the needs of excluded communities, instead of specialist providers offering 'products for the poor'.

Similarly, money transmission accounts (Basic Bank Accounts) are now offered by all of Scotland's main banks, without the facility of an overdraft or the risk of incurring charges. A government with high expectations should seek evidence of how the banks are working to stimulate demand and to increase levels of take-up of such products. Availability of appropriate products needs to be matched with a commitment to promote their use. At the same time, it is likely that new insurance products will be needed to meet emerging demands. For example, lone parents on low incomes are the least likely of any household type to benefit from financial services. There is still a clear need for basic life protection that allows small amounts of cash to be paid regularly. This adds up to a market opportunity not being addressed by the industry in any meaningful way.

While the financial services sector is highly competitive, the weight of competition is firmly skewed in favour of higher income/lower risk customers. The market to serve the already banked and insured is heavily crowded. Competition to serve those who are outside the system is weak and uneven. These households together represent lower profit but viable market opportunities, and they are being underserved by many high street providers. Key to growing these low cost markets is business working with public and voluntary sector intermediaries to share risks and benefits; to develop basic, secure products; to achieve active promotion on a high volume basis; and to organise distribution at low cost using existing channels like the Post Office and social housing providers.

With greater commitment from government and a clearer challenge to private service providers, more comprehensive cost-cutting packages could be applied to household bills for energy, food and transport. The Scottish Executive could stimulate new partnerships between smaller independent shops and the major retailers, as well as offer incentives for new businesses to set up in low-income areas. If a combined reduction of 20 per cent could be achieved on basic household bills in low-income communities,[19] this would have the same impact on disposable income as raising benefits or earnings by a similar amount. This should be seen as no more than addressing market failures in order to extend to poor communities the benefits of competition that the rest of Scotland takes for granted.

In this way, private sector services have an important role to play in extending consumer choice and reducing poverty. The engagement of banks, insurers, supermarkets, the utilities, transport providers and the Post Office should be around the shared goal of growing viable market opportunities that are currently neglected. No new subsidies are required at this stage. Instead government can bring to bear its capacity to support markets more effectively, and demonstrate how corporate social responsibility can involve core business rather than charitable works at the margins.

Progress with approaches like this would not be reflected in statistics on poverty through the Households Below Average Income (HBAI) series, however. Since income and expenditure, taken together, offer a more comprehensive account of how households are faring, a closer integration of datasets is needed, between the HBAI, the Family Resources Survey (FRS) and the Family Expenditure Survey (FES) for example.

Money

Tackling disadvantage involves more than money, but it cannot be done without it. The Government's historic ambition of abolishing child poverty within 20 years will be increasingly hard to achieve without consistent improvements in employment rates and tax/benefit changes that favour lower income households.[20] One priority for improvement is found at the start of the life cycle.

Britain continues to underinvest in the health and welfare of women during pregnancy, and in the well-being of their infants, especially in low-income families and among under-25s, despite clear improvements in family policy since 1997. Having a baby represents a key pathway into poverty for some households. The SCF's *Early endowment* study explored how families could be supported to make healthier transitions to parenthood.[21] It was based on extended group interviews with expectant mothers and mothers of young babies in two Social Inclusion Partnership areas of central Scotland[22] and group discussion with health visitors.

Participants identified the core elements of an 'ideal care and support package' during pregnancy and their children's early years. They identified their highest priority, both during pregnancy and after the baby is settled at home, as having the full support of partners and family members. Improved financial support was the second highest priority.

As well as setting their own priorities, participants responded to a number of pre-identified options for reform, based on existing policy and evidence from practice. Each was strongly supported, suggesting that women at this stage in their life would welcome *any* appropriate form of extra support.

One option is to increase incomes to help with the additional costs associated with having a baby. This builds on US evidence showing that improved birthweight and subsequent maternal and child health are associated with relatively modest supplements to income and nutrition during pregnancy. Participants consistently said that one of their biggest worries was not knowing where the money was going to come from, particularly when they were not working or were receiving less than full pay during maternity leave. Most believed that an extra £20 to £25 a week would make a significant difference to their family by reducing the sense of financial stress.

One way of achieving this objective might be to provide new mums with a 'loyalty card' to be used at supermarkets and other local shops, giving discounts on a range of baby products and perhaps 'healthy living' purchases for the parents. This approach demonstrates how purchasing power could be boosted by reducing the real cost of essential goods, as distinct from raising incomes through benefits or tax credits. Government should play a central role in promoting the loyalty card concept, and encouraging disparate parts of the retail sector to cooperate around this goal.

Another, simpler, way would be to use the existing benefits system.[23] The principle of starting to pay Child Benefit during pregnancy and at a higher rate for at least the first year is one we strongly support because of the potential physical and mental health improvements for mothers and their babies. While the Scottish Executive has no powers to alter benefit levels or phase payments differently, it could seek new ways of investing in pregnancy and infancy using other sources of funding, including the NHS and urban regeneration budgets. If effective, this approach might eventually be rolled out UK-wide through negotiation with Westminster colleagues.

Concerns that additional payments should be better integrated with advice and guidance on healthy behaviour could be addressed through alternative delivery routes: for instance, early payment could be made through the antenatal clinic. This approach might enable the related priorities of an extended health visiting service and greater peer support of other mums to be addressed more effectively.[24]

Employment
Full employment: Closing the gap
Employment levels have risen steadily in recent years. The Scottish employment rate has approached three-quarters of working age people in recent years, a stronger performance than in small neighbours like Ireland and Finland, or indeed Germany, France and Italy. Yet, with just over 60 per cent of working age people in jobs, the employment rate in Glasgow and some other urban authorities is up to 15 per cent behind the Scottish and British rates. Glasgow has remained one of Britain's biggest 'benefit cities' at a time of employment growth.

This reflects in part the fact that more people are 'on the sick' than on the dole across Britain, accounting for around 7 per cent of the workforce, and at least double this rate among men in places like Glasgow. At least 1 in 3 people on Incapacity Benefit (IB) say they would like a job, but many are fearful of doing anything that will put their benefits at risk. Expectations of working again are exceptionally low, reflecting the experiences of claimants across the UK.[25]

While recent changes in employment programmes have helped those claiming Incapacity Benefit for shorter periods, younger claimants and those living in areas of stronger jobs growth, about half of IB claimants are men aged over 50, and a growing proportion are women leaving public service employment, typically due to problems of stress and depression. For older and long-term claimants, we have found that the barriers to moving back into work tend to be formidable. They include the fear that doing any form of work could put their benefit status at risk; a continuing lack of contact between agencies and longer-term claimants; low expectations among employers as well as claimants; and a clear mismatch between claimants' conditions, which often fluctuate, and the types of jobs available.[26] If the problem of worklessness is to be addressed fully, dedicated action to tackle these barriers must be a higher priority.

Based on a series of in-depth interviews with senior decision-makers, our work on full employment set out other ambitious steps towards narrowing the gap in employment rates between the 'Glasgows of Britain' (where employment rates are little higher than 60 per cent) and the Scottish/British rates.[27] To match the British rate would mean an extra 50,000 jobless residents being in work. This requires action beyond improving programmes such as the New Deal and Employment Zones. Doubling their success rate should be a high priority, but even that might only close the gap by a third. On present trends, tens of thousands of people who could work will still be jobless without a step change in ambition.

We proposed that cities like Glasgow should aim to achieve an increase in the employment rate of residents by at least 10 per cent within five years – equivalent to another 36,000 city residents being in work. This might be achieved through additional steps to full employment, including the following:

- Significantly improving the performance of existing government initiatives such as New Deal and Employment Zones; this could result in over 12,000 jobless residents moving into sustained jobs.

- Creating an extra 3,500 local jobs by further investment in the social enterprise sector.

- Securing employer commitment through a citywide 'Working for Glasgow' initiative. This would be based on undertakings by private sector firms and public sector and community/voluntary organisations to employ and pay the wages of a jobless city resident. We suggested that 12,000 extra jobs could be created within five years. Related to this is the promotion of work sharing, through voluntary reductions in working hours among full-time employees to create new job opportunities; and intensive work at the local level in three areas[28] with employment rates as low as 40 per cent to achieve sustained work for all who want it.

- Encouraging travel outside Glasgow: jobless residents could be helped to access jobs outside the city, and ultimately to compete more effectively for future jobs created in Glasgow. This approach could open up around 3,500 job opportunities.

The shadow economy

How might small business contribute more to raising the employment rate where it is lowest? In many low-income communities, a 'shadow' economy of informal trading takes place on a cash-in-hand basis. Some activity is closely linked to drug dealing and illegal money lending. We have not explored how the links between these activities, and associated problems of violence, fear and continuing poverty, might be eroded. But we can distinguish between this and the 'grey' end of the shadow economy.

While research evidence is patchy, the 'grey' end may be characterised by a series of everyday transactions, delivering basic services such as home improvements, car repair, gardening and child care at an affordable cost. We suggest that these activities are a response to market failure. At least some of the skills and half-skills developed through such activity could be marketable in the mainstream economy. We may be more likely to grow cultures of enterprise in places where formal policy on business start-ups has so far failed by exploring whether and how some forms of 'unofficial' economic activity could be developed to become legitimate businesses, rather than treated simply as benefit fraud. Enterprise agencies, working with trusted local intermediaries, may be able to take forward this approach by changing the 'tone' of their outreach work,[29] without the need for legislative reforms first.

Time

While employment rates have risen steadily, all is not well. Through the 1990s, self-reported employee satisfaction dropped markedly in the public and private sectors. More of us are in work, but we are less happy in our jobs. The biggest causes of dissatisfaction are working hours and workload, throwing the work–life balance debate identified in *Tackling disadvantage* into sharp relief.

The SCF's new study of work–life balance issues aims to understand how lifetime working patterns are changing in the light of demographic trends.[30] We are particularly interested in exploring demand for reshaping working time across our lives, including the scope for paid and unpaid career breaks. We are considering evidence from a range of existing measures, such as the Deferred Salary Leave Programmes available to public service employees in the Canadian provinces on a contributory basis. These allow participants to take up to 1 year off on full pay after between 5 and 7 years of contributing to a sabbatical fund.

In the UK, the 'sabbatical' has been seen, traditionally, as a privilege for a small number of securely employed academics and senior professionals. Yet the concept of planned time off across the working life, over and above existing statutory entitlements,[31] is likely to have much wider appeal. There may be scope to manage the problem of 'burn-out', particularly in public service occupations, by enabling employees to take time off at various intervals in their career so that they reach the later stages of their career in better health. There may be positive implications in some sectors for job rotation and improving the skills of other employees, as well as various practical issues to be addressed in areas of staff shortage, for example.

One consequence of extending the idea of sabbaticals could be a fresh approach to how we prepare for retirement and, indeed, what we understand by that concept. For example, employees could opt to work the same number of equivalent years over a longer period, adding on each year taken in leave towards the end of their career in order to maintain the effective earning period and restore money notionally diverted from pension contributions. Such examples of 'time trading' would require a high degree of commitment from employers and rigorous evaluation to assess effects on productivity.

This issue may have particular relevance for those lifetime low earners who are among the most likely to work up to the age of claiming the state retirement pension and then to face the prospect of a low-income in retirement. There may be a strong case for government and employers to consider how low-paid employees could be give an entitlement to additional periods of time off over their working lives, through tax relief on contributions to a sabbatical fund and by having the right to borrow forward time that would otherwise not be available until retirement.

We are at the early stages of considering how the work–life balance agenda could become more relevant to all employees, including the lowest paid. The UK government has described 'asset based welfare' as a fourth pillar of welfare, in addition to work, income security and public services. This has led to proposals for a Child Trust Fund (or 'baby bond') and Savings Gateway to raise stocks of deferred income and wealth, particularly among lower income households. Our understanding of assets should now be widened to include time off across our working lives.

Trust

Disadvantaged communities often experience forms of 'network poverty' where access to job and education opportunities, for example, is restricted by constrained flows of information and practical guidance. Even when policy is changing for the better, perceptions may be slow to change because information sources are not trusted or considered credible. We have explored this issue as part of our work on long-term incapacity.[32]

The traditional assumption that people claiming long-term sickness benefits have 'worked all their days' and should be simply written off in terms of work deserves to be challenged. The greater flexibility now emerging in how fitness for work is assessed needs to be matched by a wider definition of work, including unpaid work. We have proposed a new goal for welfare reform, going beyond the Government's 'work for those who can, security for those who cannot'. We describe it as *activity for those who can be active.* One implication is that therapeutic work and volunteering should be promoted rather than merely tolerated by Jobcentre Plus and other public service agencies.

Findings from the same study showed that GPs and other primary care practitioners are strongly trusted to act in the public's best interests, while many remain suspicious of the policing role traditionally associated with the

Benefits Agency. We therefore proposed that local health centres should become information gateways, with support for GPs, other staff and trained volunteers to become more closely involved in signposting patients towards advice and forms of community activity that might help prevent their condition deteriorating. Helping people to make an active contribution in their community may be a more effective route to improving health than prescribing more medicine.

As public services become more closely integrated, we believe it will be important to expand the role of trusted intermediaries like primary care settings and schools, not least in disadvantaged neighbourhoods where people are often the most suspicious of public authorities. The principles we suggest here for older, long-term benefit claimants are of general value. Active referral using existing agencies is one way of addressing the network poverty that tends to compound other forms of disadvantage.

Conclusion

Emerging from our previous work and addressing the issues raised by the JRF's report, *Tackling disadvantage*, we favour the notion of 'active security' as a guide for action to strengthen incentives to work, learn and contribute, and to ensure that the widest possible group of people benefit from prosperity. While it is possible that very generous levels of state provision could erode initiative, it is equally true that high levels of insecurity in work and income are likely to result in people feeling defeated by change and pessimistic about the future – hardly the conditions for prosperity to be shared more widely. We cannot expect the depth, duration and concentration of poverty to be reduced in a sustainable way without carefully designed policies to offer timely support to people at times of risk. Embedded within this approach should be powerful changes within housing, neighbourhood environments and the tax and benefit systems (issues not considered in any detail here).

In this response, we have focused on some of the ways in which action can be taken to improve well-being and, crucially, longer-term prospects in poor communities and across people's lives. These have highlighted the importance of acting on many fronts, involving both reserved and devolved government powers, but also recognising the significant scope for action without the need for legislation. We have considered how various resources for tackling disadvantage could be deployed:

- Private service providers could offer more accessible, relevant and affordable products to low-income communities, with public agencies playing a more conscious role in enabling viable markets to develop.

- Money could be linked to particular times of vulnerability and to sources of advice and guidance (for instance, payment of Child Benefit during pregnancy and through antenatal clinics).

- Efforts could be stepped up to promote full employment where it is furthest from reach, including linkage of some 'shadow economy' activities into the mainstream economy where appropriate.

- There could be new forms of entitlement to improve work–life balance (for instance, time off across working lives).

- Key sources of advice on money, volunteering and jobs could be made more accessible by using trusted intermediaries as information gateways (for instance, primary care settings and schools).

Based on our analysis, we conclude with a brief comment on each of the Joseph Rowntree Foundation's four key principles to guide action.

Increase the capacity of poorer households and communities to gain from the market economy. In our view, a compounding feature of income poverty in Scotland is the failure of the market to offer effective choice on a range of goods and services (that is, choice which is accessible, affordable and relevant to needs). Public service agencies can contribute significantly to improving choice, and helping to drive down the disproportionate costs for household basics often faced by people living in low-income communities, by working more closely with private service providers to develop viable solutions in finance, retail and energy, for example.

Ensure an adequate income floor relating to what society believes are the necessities of contemporary living by minimising the number of people living in households with less than 60 per cent of median income. We would emphasise the importance of a complementary focus on the depth and duration of income poverty. For example, we need to develop better indicators of how far below the 60 per cent threshold people fall and for how long, and to what extent poverty is concentrated or dispersed geographically. The experience of living for a period of years on only 40 per cent of the median, in an impoverished neighbourhood, will be very different from spending a few months just below the poverty line in an area where most people are not poor and services are of a high quality.

Ensure that all, particularly relatively poor people and those in multiply deprived areas, have access to adequate healthcare, personal care, housing and other essential services. In our view, people with little or no ability to achieve better outcomes through moving to a better area or using their purchasing power to obtain better services should have access to the highest quality public services. Inequalities in health and learning, for example, do not simply reflect variations in public service investment, but poorer quality public services are more often found in disadvantaged communities. A more demanding principle might be based on *excellence* in public services rather than adequacy or mere availability. This means that we need broader measures of service quality to help us track progress, drawing on expertise and local intelligence that are not necessarily captured in nationally chosen indicators. We believe that the pros and cons of geographical variations in pay-setting should be considered more closely, as well as support with housing and transport costs, to help attract the most talented professionals to work in areas of greatest need.

Ensure that in the implementation of policies aimed at tackling disadvantage, there is no discrimination on the grounds of gender, race, disability, sexual orientation, religion or age. A commitment to extend prosperity to all would include a commitment to address any market or government failures which might have unintended discriminatory consequences, as well as tackling direct and intentional forms of discrimination. As part of our *Lifelines* study, we will explore how the concept of phased retirement could be extended in practice ahead of age discrimination legislation being introduced.

Notes

1   L. Boyes et al., *Out of the ordinary: The power of ambition in an uncertain world,* Scottish Council Foundation, Edinburgh, 2001.
2   Following Michael Walzer's 'spheres of justice' analysis, for example.
3   In the Strathclyde region, 27 per cent of children live in such households; D. Bell and G. Jack, *Worklessness and polarisation in Scottish households*, Scotecon, University of Stirling, 2002.
4   L. Adelman, S. Middleton, and K. Ashworth, *Britain's poorest*

children: Severe and persistent poverty and social exclusion, Save the Children/Centre for Research in Social Policy, 2003.

5   Measured as the proportion of people in households with incomes below 60 per cent of the median.

6   P. Kenway, S. Fuller, M. Rahman, C. Street and G. Palmer, *Monitoring poverty and social exclusion in Scotland,* New Policy Institute (NPI)/Joseph Rowntree Foundation, York, 2002, p. 25.

7   D. Dorling and L. Simpson, 'The geography of poverty', *New Economy* 8, no. 2 (2001), pp. 87–91.

8   Kenway et al., *Monitoring poverty,* pp. 23–4.

9   Boyes et al., *Out of the ordinary,* p. 17.

10   R. Berthoud, 'A childhood in poverty', *New Economy* 8, no. 2 (2001), pp. 77–81.

11   A. Goodman, 'Income inequality: what has happened under New Labour?', *New Economy* 8, no. 2 (2001), pp. 92–7.

12   Kenway et al., *Monitoring poverty,* p. 23.

13   For example, 1 in 4 people living on a low income in 1996 remained on a low income in each of the next 3 years, M. Rahman, G. Palmer and P. Kenway, *Monitoring poverty and social exclusion 2001,* NPI/JRF, York, 2001.

14   The causal pathways towards these outcomes are not fully understood.

15   *Possible Scotland study* (2002) for the Public Health Institute of Scotland (PHIS) and the Health Education Board for Scotland (HEBS).

16   Boyes et al., *Out of the ordinary,* and J. McCormick and G. Leicester, *Three nations: social exclusion in Scotland,* SCF, 1998, for example.

17   Both the Scottish Executive's annual *Social Justice Report* and the Department for Work and Pensions report *Opportunity for all – making progress* use this organising principle.

18   C. Whyley, J. McCormick and E. Kempson, *Paying for peace of mind: Access to home contents insurance for low-income households,* Policy Studies Institute, 1998.

19   As suggested by the Community Development Foundation.

20   H. Sutherland, T. Sefton and D. Piachaud, *Poverty in Britain: The impact of government policy since 1997,* JRF, York, 2003.

21   J. McCormick, *Early endowment: Investing better in pregnancy and infancy,* SCF, Edinburgh, 2001.

22   South Coatbridge and Inverclyde.

23 The Sure Start Maternity Grant is a targeted grant to help with the upfront costs of having a baby. While it is paid at a significantly higher rate than previous grants, there are continuing problems of awareness and take-up, and it does not address the need for additional assistance with the ongoing costs of raising a family.

24 These objectives are central features of the 'Starting Well' initiative in Glasgow, one of four public health demonstration projects led by the Scottish Executive.

25 Over a 2-year period, it is estimated that fewer than 5 per cent of people on Incapacity Benefit stop claiming because they have moved back into work.

26 J. McCormick, *On the sick: Incapacity and inclusion*, SCF, Edinburgh, 2000. The research was conducted mainly in Inverclyde, an area formerly dominated by heavy industry (including shipbuilding) and now experiencing service sector jobs growth, with a high proportion of short-term contracting.

27 B. Marshall, L. Boyes and J. McCormick, *The Full Employment City*, SCF and GCVS, Edinburgh, 2002.

28 The Full Employment Areas (FEAs) initiative.

29 To signal that their interest is in the skills and work experience developed by individuals, irrespective of how these were achieved and without such information being passed to benefits staff. An unofficial 'amnesty' might be extended to some benefit claimants who have worked without declaring earnings.

30 Findings from this study, titled 'Lifelines – re:working time', will be published in spring 2004.

31 Participants in the *Early endowment* study strongly favoured longer periods of maternity leave.

32 McCormick, *On the sick*.

5 | Community approaches to poverty in Wales

John Osmond and Jessica Mugaseth, Institute of Welsh Affairs

Looking at the present state of the Welsh economy it is possible to paint an optimistic picture of recovery and modernisation with, for example, the country rapidly moving up the UK's job creation league. Towards the end of 2003 Economic Development Minister Andrew Davies declared that since the advent of the National Assembly in 1999, Wales had 'leapfrogged' Northern Ireland, Scotland, London, the West Midlands, the North West and Yorkshire in the UK. Welsh unemployment was now lower than all these regions, placed at fourth rather than eleventh place in the league table.[1] At the same time, however, persistently high levels of economic inactivity, largely caused by chronic sickness, combine with other difficulties to place Wales at or near the top of UK statistics for poverty and disadvantage. Some of the key statistics are shown in table 5.1. Competing interpretations of economic performance and relative wealth and poverty lie at the heart of Welsh political debate and controversy.

The National Assembly was launched in 1999 at the same time as west Wales and the Valleys – about half of the country – qualified for European Union Objective One funding. While this meant that Wales stood to benefit from considerable extra investment, more than £1.3 billion over a 7-year period to 2006, it also reflected the unenviable reality that across west Wales and the Valleys – the largest Objective One area designated in the UK – gross domestic product was less than 75 per cent of the

Table 5.1 Key Welsh poverty statistics

	Wales	United Kingdom
Population, 2001 ('000s)	2,903.2	58,836.7
Percentage aged under 16	20.2	20.1
Percentage at pension age and over	20.1	18.4
Mortality rate (UK 100)	102	100
Economic inactivity (Spring 2002)	27.9%	21.5%
GDP per head (1999, UK 100)	80.5	100
Average weekly household income (1998–2001)	£376	£480
Average weekly household expenditure (1998–2001)	£315.40	£365.80
Households in receipt of Income Support (2000/01)	20%	16%
Population with household income below 60% of median income (2001/02)	25%	22% (GB)
Children living in households with income below 60% of median income (2001/02)	31%	30% (GB)
Lone parent households (2001)	7.3%	6.5%
Permanently sick or disabled (2001)	9.2%	5.8%

Source: Office for National Statistics

European average. In contrast, the eastern part of Wales – along the English border and in the north east and south east – enjoyed a GDP close to the European average.

In 1999 Welsh GDP as a whole was a little over 80 per cent of the UK average. In early policy statements the Labour-led Assembly Government declared that its underlying economic objective was to raise the figure to 90 per cent by 2010. However, this soon appeared over-ambitious since within a few years, by the beginning of the Assembly's second term, the latest available statistics were moving in the opposite direction. Wales's GDP (now referred to as 'gross value added') slipped from 79.2 per cent of the UK average in 1999, to 79 per cent in 2000, and 78.8 per cent in 2001.[2] While the UK economy as a whole, led by the more prosperous regions of the South East and Midlands, continued to grow, Wales along with the other older industrial parts of the UK grew more slowly, if at all. Inevitably the Welsh economy was slipping further behind.

Deep-seated structural problems were the widely acknowledged cause. As is well known, during the 1970s and 1980s Wales lost most of the jobs in coal and steel that had largely sustained its economy during the twentieth century. Employment in coal mining, which stood at more than 100,000 in the mid 1950s, fell to less than 2,000 by the mid 1990s. The collapse of the steel industry happened later but faster, from 72,000 employed in 1980 to a little over 16,000 by the mid 1990s. These jobs were largely replaced by a remarkable growth in manufacturing and the service sector in the last two decades of the century. However, many of these jobs were part-time, to a large extent substituted women for men and were generally less well paid.

In the late 1990s and the first few years of the new century yet another wave of structural change took place. Between 1998 and 2002 Wales lost some 44,000 manufacturing jobs in the private sector as inward investment declined and jobs moved to eastern Europe, north Africa and the Far East where wage rates were far cheaper. In the same period these losses were more than compensated for by the creation of 67,000 jobs in public administration, overwhelmingly in health and education. In 2002, 32 per cent of Welsh employment was in public administration, well ahead of any other UK economic region. The North East was closest, with 29 per cent, while the figures for London, the South East, East and East Midlands were more distant at 23 per cent. The overall result has been that Wales has exchanged higher value-adding, higher productivity, export-earning jobs for, by and large, jobs likely to be increasingly reliant on financial transfers from Whitehall. As Phil Cooke, Director of the Centre for Advanced Studies, at Cardiff University, has put it:

> *Under devolution, due to an absence of visionary policy making to tackle changed global economic realities, Wales is becoming more dependent not less on London for the underwriting of its economic future. As a precaution against rising net job loss the Assembly Government has used its own block grant resources, growing as UK expenditure on health and education burgeons, to increase employment rapidly in those sectors plus direct public administration ... Wales seems to have brought forth a new model of job-generation, the nearest predecessor of which may be that practised by Gosplan, the Soviet Union's economic development agency.[3]*

From the point of view of poverty and disadvantage, an even more fundamental problem is on the supply side of the Welsh economy. For instance, around one in ten of young people leave Welsh schools and colleges without any qualifications. By GCSE stage only around 50 per cent achieve A–C grades in English and just 40 per cent in maths. The source of this problem is simple reading and writing, the fact that large numbers of Welsh people – at all ages – perform poorly in these, literally, basic skills. As Kevin Morgan, Director of the Regeneration Institute at Cardiff University, has remarked: 'One wonders if we have the skills to enter the knowledge economy when one in four of the population is functionally illiterate and one in three functionally innumerate.'[4]

Underlying these imbalances is an even more intractable concentration of localised difficulties in the south Wales Valleys. Their unique combination of high economic inactivity rates, high morbidity, low educational achievement, and an ingrained cultural homogeneity separate them from the rest of Wales, let alone the rest of the United Kingdom. In fact, the Valleys completely distort the Welsh policy agenda. There is no doubt that if their problems were tackled on a systematic basis, and their range of dismal statistics brought closer to the Welsh average, then the salience of Wales as a hot spot for poverty and disadvantage in the UK would be much reduced, if not eliminated altogether.

The Assembly Government's approach

In its first term the Assembly Government increasingly aligned itself with the social exclusion agenda, a position it emphasised in the run-up to the May 2003 election. Its approach was articulated most clearly by the First Minister Rhodri Morgan in what became known as his 'clear red water' address at the end of 2002. In it, he drew attention to a philosophical distinctiveness between *Welsh* and *New* Labour:

Our commitment to equality leads directly to a model of the relationship between the government and the individual which regards that individual as a citizen rather than as a consumer. Approaches which prioritise choice over equality of outcome rest, in the end, upon a market approach to public services, in which individual economic actors pursue their own best interests with little regard for wider considerations.[5]

Rhodri Morgan argued that a key theme in the first four years of the Assembly had been the creation of a new set of citizenship rights which, as far as possible, were free at the point of use, universal and unconditional. He then listed five examples where the Assembly Government had introduced free services to provide individuals with an enhanced sense that they were stakeholders in society:

- Free school milk for the youngest children.
- A free nursery place for every 3 year old.
- Free prescriptions for young people in the age range 16–25.
- Free entry to museums and galleries for all citizens.
- Free local bus travel for pensioners and disabled people.

Services that were reserved for the poor, he added, very quickly become poor services. Two symbolic commitments appeared in Welsh Labour's May 2003 election manifesto. These were the abolition of prescription charges (albeit that more than 80 per cent of prescriptions were already free) and the provision of free breakfasts for children in primary schools.

In administrative terms, the most significant innovation in his cabinet after the election was the new position of Minister for Social Justice and the appointment of former

Finance Minister Edwina Hart to the post. Rhodri Morgan described the new portfolio as representing the central challenge facing his administration in its second term. As he put it, 'We've got to deliver for the people in Wales who've got left behind and where the new prosperity has not reached them.'[6]

Edwina Hart's main weapon in tackling deprivation is the administration's flagship *Communities First* programme, aimed at tackling the deprivation concentrated largely within the Objective One region of rural west Wales and the old industrial south Wales Valleys.[7] Involving expenditure of £83 million over the first three years (2002–5), the programme is targeting 142 of Wales's most disadvantaged communities. It has a lifespan of at least 10 years with the long-term intention of tackling the underlying factors that contribute to poverty. It is intended, too, that the communities themselves, in partnership with statutory bodies, voluntary groups and the private sector, will identify their requirements and how to address them. Capacity building – that is, building leadership from within the communities themselves – forms a central part of this strategy.

Few would quarrel with any of these objectives, but the challenge will be to put in place practical measures to ensure they are delivered. Mrs Hart's appointment can be understood in terms of the administration's recognition of this challenge. There are at least three further, interrelated problems. First, the Assembly Government's Economic Development division was not centrally involved in the development of the programme. Instead it was motivated by Edwina Hart's Communities department. This is despite the programme's underlying purpose of tackling economic inactivity rates, and in turn addressing the Assembly Government's core objective of raising overall Welsh GDP from 80 per cent to 90 per cent of the UK average by 2010.

Secondly, the main agents for the delivery of *Communities First* are local authorities. These are the organisations to which money is flowing and which are doing the recruiting. Yet a central aim of the project is to build leadership capacity from within the affected communities. While local authorities are theoretically representative of the communities because of their democratically elected position, they are often distrusted because of their previously poor service provision to deprived communities. There is a danger that the programme's objective of building capacity might end up with communities becoming alienated from the process.[8]

Finally, it is not clear what the programme's precise targets are, or how they will be evaluated. How can 'capacity building' be assessed? It is the case that in April 2003 the Assembly Government commissioned a large-scale Evaluation Project, worth around £1 million. However, this will not report for some years. In short, it is not that the policy being adopted is inherently wrong or misguided. Rather, it is that there is little sense of how it will be delivered effectively on the ground and thereby make a real difference.

This is also the case in other policy areas that have the potential to make a large impact on social exclusion across Wales. Another example is the Assembly Government's Basic Skills Strategy. Launched in April 2001, it will have cost £27 million by April 2004. However, by the end of this period it is far from clear:

- how its impact will be assessed; or
- how future improvements will be made in pursuing what must be a long-term policy commitment.

The Assembly Government did commission an evaluation programme in early 2003, but the results will be delivered

119

too late to have any impact on the delivery of the Strategy's first 3-year period. Despite such criticisms, an analysis of Assembly Government policy initiatives reveals a determination to devise special programmes and allocate available budgets to assist those most at risk. The following provides evidence of a concerted determination to back up Welsh Labour rhetoric with positive interventions.

The family

The incidence of child poverty in Wales is among the highest in the UK. In 2000/01, 33 per cent of children in Wales lived in households with incomes below half mean income after housing costs, compared with 30 per cent in Great Britain.[9] In its first term, the Assembly Government established a cabinet subcommittee on Children and Young People to give a lead on children's and young people's issues. This was complemented by a Child Poverty Task Group charged with developing a strategy for combating child poverty in Wales. Following extensive consultations this is due to be published in September 2004.

As part of its strategy in 2003–4 the Assembly Government created a unified grant fund known as *Cymorth* ('Help') to bring together under one umbrella £39 million (during the first year) from various funding strands. Part of this money is being used for childcare provision to enable parents to work or attend training schemes. This strikes directly against economic inactivity, which is often at the heart of child poverty.

The Assembly Government has also resolved that investment in early years' education is an effective way of tackling both child deprivation and the deficit in basic skills. Two initiatives stand out. Firstly, every 3 year old in Wales should have the opportunity to receive free half-time education by 2004. The Assembly Government provided £12 million in 2002/03 towards this objective and commissioned an audit to identify current provision and estimates of future demand in Wales across all sectors. Secondly, each Local Authority is to develop at least one pilot, integrated early years centre by September 2004. These centres will provide 'wrap-around' day-care together with a range of support services from pre-natal parenting through to adult learning. Integrated centres will seek to tackle wider social problems in Wales such as child poverty and those arising from a relatively high proportion of teenage mothers. They will be jointly funded by local authorities' social services and education budgets.

Teenage pregnancy and lone parents

Closely related to child poverty is the relatively high prevalence of teenage pregnancy and single parenthood in Wales. Although the incidence of teenage pregnancy is beginning to decline, Wales still has some of the highest figures in Europe, ranging from 42 conceptions per 1,000 in Monmouth to over 91 in Caerphilly. These compare with an English average of 44 per 1,000 in 2000.[10] Overall, rates of teenage pregnancy are highest in the areas of greatest deprivation and among the most vulnerable young people, including those in care and those who have been excluded from school. The Assembly Government responded early on, launching a Strategic Framework for Promoting Sexual Health in Wales in 2000, with the main objective of reducing teenage pregnancy.

Carers

Census figures indicate that 11.7 per cent of the Welsh population (340,700 people) provide unpaid care compared with 9.9 per cent in England. Of these 26.3 per cent (20.5 per cent in England) provide 50 or more hours of care per week. As part of its Carers' Strategy the Assembly

Government allocated an extra £4.6 million to local authorities in 2002/03 for enhanced support to carers.

Long-term illness

The latest figures show that 23.3 per cent of the Welsh population have a limiting long-term illness compared with 17.9 per cent in England. In fact, the English figure is even below the lowest local authority percentage in Wales; Cardiff with 18.8 per cent. With 30 per cent, Merthyr has the dubious distinction of the highest rate. Wales also has a significantly higher proportion of the population who are permanently sick or disabled; almost double the UK average of 5.3 per cent, at 9.2 per cent.[11] The Assembly Government is planning to abolish home care charges for disabled people, ensuring that people can afford care in their own homes.

The elderly

At the other end of the demographic scale, Wales is also facing mounting problems with an ageing population. The age distribution of the population in Wales differs from that for the UK with a higher proportion of people in retirement age; a trend set to continue. It is predicted that those above retirement age will increase by 11 per cent to nearly 650,000 in 2021 (continuing to rise thereafter).[12] This increase in the elderly population will put pressure not only on the benefit system but also the healthcare structure. At the same time places in local authority homes in Wales declined by 36 per cent between 1991 and 2001, to 4,534 places.[13]

Recognising these changing demographics, in January 2003 the Assembly Government produced *A Strategy for Older People* which complements the UK's *Better Government for Older People*. This 10-year programme identifies a number of strategic aims and objectives, provides a policy rationale and outlines an implementation plan to take forward more detailed actions and projects. The Assembly Government is also establishing a cabinet subcommittee to ensure a continued and coherent focus on the needs of older people. A national partnership forum for older people is being introduced to ensure that progress on the strategy is monitored and that older people and their representatives have a voice at national level. The Assembly Government's most recent strategy document, *Wales: A better country,* published in September 2003, contains a commitment to appoint a commissioner to ensure that the needs of older people are reflected in services and policy.

Housing

Housing in Wales is substantially older than the rest of the United Kingdom, with 35 per cent of homes built before 1919, compared with only 21 per cent in England.[14] Much of this stock is in poor condition, with a higher unfitness rate in Wales than in England. In 2001 the Assembly Government published a National Housing Strategy aimed at bringing all social housing in the country up to a new Welsh Housing Quality Standard by 2012. In addition in 2002/04 £3.2 million was given to care and repair agencies to enable older and disabled people to carry out improvements to their homes.

Development by community

From a Welsh perspective the Joseph Rowntree Foundation's paper *Tackling disadvantage: A 20-year enterprise* comes across as a highly Anglocentric document. This is not to suggest that its overview and analysis are poorly judged; and nor is its main prescription that, with modest adjustments, the UK government's expenditure patterns could go a long way to reduce poverty. Rather, it is that the perspective tends to concentrate on the predicament of individuals within society rather than with society itself. That is to say, problems are addressed in terms of lone mothers, children at risk, the disabled, or the elderly living on their own, and solutions are formulated accordingly. An alternative approach is to consider first the wider context of the communities within which disadvantaged people live, and to see how the collective condition can be improved.

This is typically the Welsh starting point, which stresses a more holistic approach to the communities within which individuals have to find ways of improving their life chances. And this is despite the continual difficulty that many individuals may be alienated from the communities within which they are fated to live. It is no accident that the main Assembly Government programme designed to engage with social exclusion is entitled *Communities First.* Indeed, Welsh policy makers have been very precise in identifying the 142 communities that qualify according to the multiple index of deprivation. Of course, Wales has more than its fair share of people within the categories of deprivation identified in the Rowntree report, as the analysis earlier in this chapter has demonstrated. However, the instinctive Welsh view is both to describe problems and think of solutions in terms of the needs of communities as a whole. This may simply be a response to the smaller and therefore more intimate scale of Welsh society. It probably also reflects that when thinking about their identity the Welsh tend to associate themselves in the first instance with their immediate locality – their town, village or valley (the Welsh language term is *bro*) – rather than with Wales as a whole.

In this respect, it is worth highlighting three initiatives: one in the south Wales Valleys, another in rural Wales, and the third covering Wales as a whole. If taken up on a wider scale these would certainly assist in addressing social deprivation in Wales in the next 20 years.

Gellideg, Merthyr

The first initiative is in Merthyr, which is one of the most severely deprived local authorities in Wales and the whole of the UK (see Box 5.1 below). Faced with this catalogue of deprivation – a common picture across the Heads of the Valleys – it is tempting to throw up one's hands in despair. Yet the beginnings of a response have been discovered within the community itself, from the run-down Gellideg estate in Merthyr. This story is of how a group of people with few resources and little formal education came to build a real community.

Today they have their own organisation, the Gellideg Foundation, which has raised more than £700,000 (including a successful bid for £500,000 Objective One funding) and now has a staff of 13. With these resources they have provided job training, restored and equipped community buildings, created an outdoor sports area, a café and a crèche, and employed their own community workers. In the process they have analysed the power structures within the estate and the world beyond and come to understand some of the problems that have been holding them back.[15] It is a story of genuine empowerment from below, to which, as we have seen, the *Communities First* programme aspires. If the programme is to be successful, it needs to draw on the lessons provided by the Gellideg Foundation and apply them across Wales.

One interesting learning point from the Gellideg project has been the contrasting attitudes of men and women to their circumstances and the need for policy makers to respond. It has shown that a failure to apply a gender perspective – being in effect 'gender blind' – means that policy interventions can unconsciously reinforce gender

---

Box 5.1 **Merthyr's poverty statistics**

- 66 per cent of households have an income of less than £10,000
- 48.6 per cent are in employment
- 28 per cent of households are in receipt of Housing Benefit
- 29 per cent per cent of housing is local authority or housing association owned
- 13.6 per cent of households are occupied by lone parents
- 12.5 per cent of homes are 'not fit for habitation'
- 44 per cent of people aged between 16 and 60 have no qualifications
- 30 per cent suffer from limiting long-term illness

Source: Assembly Government, *Mapping social exclusion in Wales,* 1999; 2001 census

---

stereotyping. So, for example, pre-school provision becomes in practice a mother and toddler group, thereby excluding men. Such stereotyping limits the life choices available to men and women and can reinforce inequalities. Many such messages emerged from the Gellideg survey. For example, the following attitudes to employment were reported:

> *Unemployment for men is seen as the norm ... Many younger men show a strong desire to start their own business. When explored further, this desire often comes from a fear of being unemployable by others, sometimes because of the stigma of being an ex-offender. Lack of business experience and little knowledge of finances are the primary obstacles to pursing this interest. Young men also feel that factories are likely to take on women ahead of men because women are cheaper to employ ... Older men feel on the margins of the economy, believing that*

there is little point in retraining and that it would be humiliating to do so. Their perception is that the computer-literate young get the chances, and that their own plentiful experience in both formal and informal employment is not valued in the job market.

Women need to find employment that fits around the needs of their children. On the whole men do not take a part in childcare responsibilities. Women caring for children look for job opportunities that fit around school hours – these jobs are invariably low-paid and part-time and do not make going to work pay ... Young women feel that the lack of sound advice is preventing them from accessing training, education and employment opportunities ... It is felt by all groups that everyone is struggling to survive. One woman said: 'When everything has been paid out on the household I have about £20 a fortnight left. When food or other necessities are short I just go without.'[16]

The messages emerging from Gellideg have informed the many campaigning organisations in Wales that address poverty questions. For instance, at the time of the May 2003 Assembly elections, Anti-Poverty Network Cymru urged the parties to put poverty questions higher up their agenda, and in particular to:

- ensure that anti-poverty policy development is informed and led by those in poverty – essential if it is to be successful in countering social exclusion;
- ensure that local government becomes more accountable and participatory in its approach;
- introduce participatory budgeting in Wales – a powerful

mechanism which enables local people to determine the allocation of budgets in their area;

- involve people living in poverty in the monitoring and evaluation of anti-poverty measures.[17]

Rural Wales

The second initiative highlighted here, which proposes a radical rethinking of spatial planning in rural Wales, also relates to the 'Unequal places' section of the JRF *Tackling disadvantage* report. Islands of poverty, often isolated and because of that cut off from prospects of revival, are to be found across the Welsh hinterland. The need, therefore, is for all parts of rural Wales to have a relationship with a nearby urban settlement. An important study, produced by the Centre for Enterprise and Rural Development at the University of Wales, Bangor, has identified around a dozen such 'development domains' in rural Wales and proposed a sustainable development strategy linked to them.[18]

The main argument is that development priority should be given to key centres in rural Wales to counter the magnetic attraction of southern Wales, and in particular Cardiff. It is a radical response to the widely recognised need for a distribution of investment and economic activity from the wealthier parts of mainly urban Wales to the rest of the country. Typically, the expensively produced Assembly Government's *Spatial Plan for Wales* acknowledges this but fails to come up with a targeted strategy. Instead, it relies on declaratory injunctions.[19] In contrast, the Bangor proposal envisages the establishment of a special fund to be administered by Regeneration Authorities for each of the 'development domains' it suggests. These will comprise existing settlements in rural Wales combined with the ports of Holyhead and Fishguard – hence the term 'domain' to describe them. A strategic approach for each of these 'domains' should include:

- their development as regional growth centres;
- investment in urban renewal programmes and in projects to fill in infrastructure deficits;
- investment in their education institutions – or the creation of institutions where they do not exist;
- designation of as many of them as possible as a national centre for some activity – for example e-commerce in Milford Haven and software in Bangor;
- building on their existing attributes to attract inward investment, linking local enterprise with education institutions;
- developing tourism in their surrounding hinterlands with facilities that could service both tourism and local market needs;
- upgrading communication links between them and the main urban centres in north and south Wales;
- decentralising Assembly Government departments, for example Agriculture to Aberystwyth, the Roads Division to Bangor; and Assembly-sponsored public bodies, for example the Arts Council of Wales to Carmarthen and the Environment Agency to Dolgellau.

By themselves such policy proposals are not especially original. However, taken together, and placed within the context of a new spatial strategy for rural Wales, they are highly challenging to established thinking. The potential for utilising Objective One investment is obvious. Undoubtedly, the notion of focusing investment in such specifically designated 'domains' will generate controversy. What, it will be asked, is to happen to those majority locations in rural Wales that are not chosen as part of such a strategy? The answer is that a growth pole approach along these lines would assist rural Wales as a whole. Certainly a radical approach is needed if the intractable problems of rural Wales are to be addressed systematically.

And in any event, locations with natural advantages tend to develop anyway. Unplanned, however, they remain unfocused and do not develop to optimum advantage.

Community Enterprise Wales

The third community development initiative we have chosen to highlight focuses on the work of Community Enterprise Wales, established a decade ago as a spin-out, social economy networking organisation from the Welsh Development Agency. Since that time the organisation has helped establish more than 400 groups across Wales which, taken together, have created a recognisable social economy in the country. For many disadvantaged communities, developing the social economy is the best, and perhaps the only opportunity for generating economic activity.

On many of Wales's so-called 'sink' estates there are models of economic development in being that are helping residents of all ages address their own identified social and economic needs. As we have seen with the Gellideg example above, they are being developed in partnership with the various 'communities' within the estates, based on lifestyle and gender-specific interests, recognising diversity and not treating an estate as a homogeneous whole. They begin by letting the consumers decide what services they want, where and by whom they should be delivered, at prices they can afford. As one research paper from Community Enterprise Wales puts it:

> *Contrary to the popular myths that have arisen around estates like Ely and St Mellons (in Cardiff), Gurnos (in Merthyr), and Penrhys (in the Rhondda), the vast majority of people want opportunities to get into jobs, earn money and contribute. They don't want, or respond*

*positively to, patronising development strategies.
Enterprise in its widest sense is illustrated across
these estates. To quote one Gurnos resident
'people have to be enterprising to live'.[20]*

Strategies are being developed which have the potential
to:

- contribute to local regeneration;
- mix commercial and public finance in creative ways to
  increase investment in deprived communities;
- combine market opportunity with better access to
  services;
- challenge the traditional roles and boundaries between
  public, private and the community across Wales.

However, the full potential of Community Enterprise Wales
has yet to be realised. For instance, its work has not been
mainstreamed in the *Communities First* initiative, a glaring
omission which will need to be rectified if the Assembly
Government's flagship policy for addressing disadvantage
is to have the impact it deserves.

Conclusion

Pockets of extreme poverty exist throughout Wales, with
the south Wales Valleys a particular problem area both for
the numbers involved and the extent and range of
deprivation. Other concentrations exist along parts of the
north Wales coastline, in Holyhead on Anglesey, in south
Pembrokeshire around Milford Haven and Pembroke, and
in certain wards in Cardiff, Newport and Swansea, as well
as in a number of rural areas.

The problems in the Valleys are complex, and result from
the failure of many communities to adapt to the loss of
jobs in traditional sectors such as coal and steel, and more

recently to the decline in manufacturing industry. This has left a legacy of reported ill-health, low skill levels and aspirations, and consequently low employment activity rates. On the surface, unemployment appears to have reached tolerably low levels, but when combined with sickness and disability claimants the proportions not working are higher than virtually anywhere else in the UK. For example, more than 30 per cent of the population in both Merthyr Tydfil and Blaenau Gwent are claiming benefits of one kind or another, compared with just under 20 per cent for Wales as a whole. In both cases, too, more than 20 per cent are registered as sick or disabled. This last compares with a Welsh figure of 13.3 per cent.

In some Valley communities the number of households without an adult in employment is approaching 50 per cent and the proportion of pupils claiming free school meals in some authorities is more than 50 per cent higher than in Wales generally. Other factors leading to higher levels of poverty in parts of Wales, including the Valleys, are the large number of single parents and young parents.

Partly also reflecting the loss of what were well paid, if hard, jobs in traditional industries and their replacement, if at all, by lower paid work in manufacturing, food processing and service industries, average weekly earnings for those in work are significantly lower in the poorer parts of Wales both for men and women. Men in the Rhondda secure 92 per cent of Welsh average gross weekly earnings (with Wales itself well below the UK figure). Access to vehicles, a key to finding employment in areas with poor public transport facilities, is also lower in many parts of Wales, including the Valleys, than in the rest of the UK.

The location and scale of these problems mean that they are unlikely to be addressed by the conventional means of attracting inward investment or persuading private firms, whether in the manufacturing or service sectors, to move in and provide jobs. In the first instance the challenge is to create a greater range of social capital by developing the social economy. Only then will there be a realistic chance of putting in place the more normal mix of private, public and voluntary sector activity that characterises less disadvantaged parts of the country. In rural Wales the message is in part the same. But here there is the additional challenge of creating communities of such critical mass that they can attract the full range of employment and lifestyle opportunities that people have the right to expect. This is the rationale behind the development domains approach sketched out above.

Wales has a formidable amount of poverty and deprivation to address, more than most other parts of the United Kingdom. However, it also has a political leadership highly sensitive to the challenge and a determination to try and address it. Perhaps more important even than that, Wales has a latent strength in its powerful sense of community which holds out the potential of producing long-term, community-based solutions.

Notes

1   Andrew Davies, 'Jobs to rejoice over', *Western Mail*, 13 September 2003. He reported: 'The number of economically inactive people who want a job has fallen by a quarter during the Assembly's first term. At the same time the level of economic activity has increased by 67,000 and we have cut in half the economic activity gap between Wales and the UK as a whole.'

2   'Wales slips further in UK wealth table', *Western Mail*, 21 August 2003.

3   Phil Cooke, 'Economic governance: Scotland's visionary and Wales's precautionary approach', in John Osmond (ed.), *Second term challenge: Can the Welsh Assembly Government hold its course?*, Institute of Welsh Affairs, November 2003 page 28.

4   Kevin Morgan, 'Over-worked, under-resourced and unloved', *Agenda,* journal of the Institute of Welsh Affairs, Autumn 2001, an assessment of the first two years of the National Assembly.

5   Rhodri Morgan, speech to the National Centre for Public Policy, University of Wales, Swansea, 11 December 2002.

6   *Welsh Mirror*, 10 May 2003.

7   For an analysis of the origins and development of the programme, see Dave Adamson and Eilidh Johnston, 'Communities First', in J. Osmond and J. B. Jones (eds), *Birth of Welsh democracy: the first term of the National Assembly for Wales*, Institute of Welsh Affairs, 2003.

8   Attention was drawn to this by Barbara Castle, one of Edwina Hart's advisers in drawing up the strategy. As she put it, *Communities First* 'was meant to be a "bottom up" project rather than a "top down" one. Things have not worked out that way', *Western Mail*, 29 August 2003.

9   National Statistics, *Statistical Bulletin, Child Poverty*, SB43/2002, May 2002.

10   Office for National Statistics.

11   Census 2001.

12   Government Actuary's Department 2001-based interim population projections for Wales.

13   See www.lgdu-wales.gov.uk.

14   *Welsh housing statistics 2002*, April 2003; *English House Condition Survey 2001*, July 2003.

15   For a fuller description of how the Gellideg Foundation came into being and operates see Helen Buhaenko, 'Combating the gender contract', *Agenda*, IWA Spring 2003. See also an Oxfam Cymru report on the project, *Fifty voices are better than one: Combating social exclusion and gender stereotyping in Gellideg in the South Wales Valleys*, April 2003, available from Oxfam Cymru, Market Buildings, St Mary Street, Cardiff CF10 1AT.

16   *Agenda*, IWA, Spring 2003.

17   Anti-Poverty Network Cymru, *A call for an outward looking Wales*, May 2003. The network comprises Amnesty International Wales, CAFOD, Christian Aid, Cyfanfyd – The Development Education Association for Wales, Displaced People In Action, Friends of the Earth Cardiff, Friends of the Earth Cymru, Help the Aged Cymru, Minority Ethnic Women's Network – MEWN Cymru, The National Group on Homeworking, Oxfam Cymru, Refugee Media Group in Wales, Save the Children/Tearfund, UNA Wales, VSO Wales, The Wales Fair Trade Forum, Wales Women's National

Coalition, Welsh Food Alliance, Welsh Centre for International Affairs, Welsh Refugee Council, Womankind, WWF Cymru.

18 Gareth Wyn Jones and Einir Young, *A bright future for rural Wales: An approach to securing greater economic and social justice within Wales and between Wales and the rest of the UK and the EU and to moving towards a more sustainable future*, Working Paper no. 1, Centre for Enterprise and Regional Development, University of Wales, Bangor, April 2003. See also their 'Rural revival strategy', *Agenda*, IWA Spring 2003.

19 Welsh Assembly Government, *People, places, futures: The Wales Spatial Plan*, October 2003.

20 Community Enterprise Wales, *Strategic regeneration: A role for enterprising communities*, April 2002.